Forest
School
Handbook

Forest
School
Handbook

Naomi Walmsley & Dan Westall

Contents

Introduction

Packed full of practical ideas for getting kids outside, this book is your essential companion for helping them play, craft and learn about the natural world around us. Make fire by rubbing sticks together, build a shelter to sleep under, create stone tools using scavenged materials, make natural glue from tree sap, harvest clay from the earth to make pots, turn common garden weeds into delicious and nourishing wild food, and much more.

Forest School activities are designed to help children thrive in our natural environment, learning how to enjoy and make use of wild spaces. They can help develop practical skills, like cooking on a campfire, making dens and crafting using natural materials. Younger children can enjoy the simpler exercises with their parents and older children can discover new skills on their own.

Our passion is to connect people to nature through skill acquisition and play. We believe that all children (and adults!) should be able to light a fire (safely) by the age of ten, know at least ten different uses for a stick and a stone, recognize at least five of the plants and trees they see daily, and be able to identify at least ten different birds. It is our mission, through this book, to enable them to do that.

Living as hunter-gatherers

We have been teaching in the outdoors for many years, but some of our greatest learning experiences, which have shaped the way we live and teach today, have been wilderness adventures: one in eastern Washington, USA, for five months and a month filming for a TV series in a remote part of Bulgaria. Both times we lived as primitive hunter-gatherers, learning the skills of our Stone Age ancestors, including hunting, fishing and preparing the buckskin used to make our clothes. We foraged, crafted, preserved, pickled and dried, practised making fire and sculpted tools from rocks and bones. We had no phones, electricity, maps or sat nav, no chocolate or sugar, and no tent. We had only the food we foraged, the clothes we had made and the stars in the sky as our roof and our guide. Living out in the wild with no modern equipment gave us a new perspective on life and we have some truly special stories of these primitive living experiences that we use to inspire both adults and children.

Playing in nature

Increasingly, we look back to compare our childhoods to the way things are for children now. We would complain to our parents that we had 'nothing to do', reluctantly dragging ourselves outside, complaining of being too tired to play, yet would entertain ourselves for hours, roaming around until the sun went down or dinner was ready, whichever came first. We would collect snails, build ramps, hunt for the hairiest caterpillars and dig for treasure (things we still do). When we finally came back in, we would be ravenously hungry, full of stories, enthusiastically planning future projects and completely re-energized.

Abundant research confirms that interacting with nature can nurture creativity, promote good health, raise vitamin levels, inspire problem-solving and build confidence. Nature can be both a playground and a classroom, as well as a vast storehouse of things to eat and to build with. Some early encounters with nature are rites of passage: discovering the joys of stomping and splashing in puddles, building sandcastles, or releasing a cloud of fluffy parachutes by blowing on a dandelion seedhead. With these discoveries come important never-to-be-forgotten lessons, such as what happens when the muddy puddle is deeper than the height of your wellies, or what happens when you build that sandcastle too close to the tide line!

Positive impacts of playing outside:

- Promotes well-being.
- Develops muscle strength and helps with coordination.
- Boosts self-confidence and creative thinking.
- Burns extra calories, which will help prevent obesity.
- Promotes good sleep and a healthy appetite.
- Exposes us to sunlight, which makes us feel happier.

As children grow older, their interactions with nature become more complex and create more learning opportunities: close encounters with a bramble bush allow them to experience the bliss of a ripe blackberry as well as the sharp prickle of thorns. The four-year-old who keeps a ladybird as a pet in a matchbox may be inconsolable when she discovers it has died, but begins an understanding about loss, grief and habitat, which will last a lifetime. And there's no need to convince someone of the value of identifying a dock leaf or plantain once they have been stung by a nettle. There are so many positive interactions with nature that could benefit adults and children throughout their life, if they are encouraged from a young age.

Unfortunately, many of our green spaces have given way to houses and roads. Fear makes some parents unsure about letting children roam too far. But nature doesn't always mean big woodlands or green parks. It can be in our back gardens or on our front doorsteps. Although the independence of roaming free is appealing to most children, these experiences can be just as fun shared with parents or siblings. Our hope is that this book can act as a guide to allow these connections to take place.

NATURE AWARENESS

Everywhere you look in nature there is learning potential. We only need to look to the creatures of the forest to learn about being masters of camouflage, to the sky to learn about peripheral vision, or observe our nocturnal friends to learn about epic night vision. We can use our powers of observation and detective skills to find out more about nature and discover the fascinating secrets of the natural world.

Minibeast hunting

There's a tiny world out there that most of us know nothing about – a world where the bugs and beasts of the underground and overground go about their everyday chores: finding food, storing food, finding cover and mostly concentrating on not getting eaten by something bigger. Why not go on a hunt to find some of these creepy-crawlies?

AGE Any
TIME 5+ minutes
TOOLS None
MATERIALS Collecting pots, magnifying glass

Think where you would hide if you were a bug trying to hide away or have a sleep. Look in the nooks and crannies of trees, under logs and in hedges. Where would you go if you were a slug or snail and wanted to find a cold, dark, damp place to chill out? If you have a magnifying glass you can get up close but it's amazing what our naked eyes can see, too, when we really look hard.

1

Make sure you put all the bugs back where you found them.

2

Muddy tracks

Tracking can mean many different things. To me, it is about being a detective, searching for clues, taking in evidence and making a story of what happened. Who was here? What did they do? You could find a footprint, a hoof mark or claw marks. You could find scattered feathers, a collection of nutshells, or even a bit of fur or bones. Here is a simple way of developing your observation skills. Sand works well to begin with as you can clearly see tracks in it.

AGE 5+
GROUP SIZE 2+
TIME 5+ minutes
TOOLS None
MATERIALS Mud or sand, long sticks for the edges of the pit

Step 1

Create a pit at least 3 x 2ft (90 x 60cm) by laying out sticks to form the edges. The bigger the pit, the better the tracks will be. Fill the pit with mud or sand. Working one at a time in pairs or small groups, one person will decide how to move through the pit. They could run, hop or jump; move slowly or quickly; heavy-footed or lightly. While the other partner or rest of the group isn't looking, this person moves through the tracking pit in the chosen style.

Step 2

The others must now work out how it was done by looking at the tracks made. Look closely at the depth and width of track. Did the mud or sand move anywhere else? Come up with an answer and talk about the results.

Story tracks

In small groups (a minimum of three groups works best), collect items from around you, such as a phone, keys, clothes, tools or food. Decide on a simple story. Make tracks in your pit to fit your scenario and scatter the items around the pit. Ask a new group to come in and work out what happened. Who was here? How fast or slow were they moving? Behave like detectives and try to figure out each scenario.

Sit spot

The idea of spending ten minutes in a woodland, meadow or garden, sitting quietly and soaking up the atmosphere, is close to my idea of heaven. This is what we call a 'sit spot'. For toddlers, teenagers and fully fledged grown-ups, a sit spot is a great activity. Yes, it's a good excuse to be pardoned from chores or homework, but it is also an opportunity to develop a deep connection to nature.

AGE Any
TIME Up to 20 minutes
TOOLS None
MATERIALS None

Find a tree or other comfortable place and sit for anywhere between 5–20 minutes. Put your peripheral vision into practice and try to be still and observe the world around you. How long you sit for is not important. It's a good idea to choose the same place each time to give you a chance to get to know your spot. You will notice changes, like new tracks, and observe the habits of the creatures that share the area with you. Your spot could even be at the bottom of your garden or on your front doorstep.

Things to look and listen for:

- What plants grow there.
- Spiders weaving webs.
- Birdsong, bird alarm calls and other noises.
- Squirrels burying or digging for nuts.
- Animal tracks.
- Animal's fur transferred onto twigs.
- Bark rubbed off trees, indicating deer rubbing their antlers.
- Birds collecting materials for nests.
- Ants doing busy collecting work.

Flour trail tracker

While out hunting, a group of hunters manage to shoot a mammoth with a bow and arrow, but unfortunately only injure him. The mammoth escapes into the bush, leaving a trail of blood behind him. The hunters are now on a tight timeframe to find the mammoth before he gets too far away. This activity creates an exciting atmosphere in which the participants are encouraged to use their observation skills and tune into their senses as well as their environment.

AGE 6+

TIME 15+ minutes

TOOLS Walkie-talkie radios are desirable but not essential

MATERIALS Flour, camouflage paint (optional)

Split into two teams. Name one group the 'mammoth' and the other the 'hunters'. Give each group walkie-talkies if you have them. The mammoth group has two minutes to get away (depending on the size of the area and the boundaries set, you may want to vary the time allowance).

The mammoth group members travel in a line, one behind the other. The person at the front sprinkles a handful of flour to symbolize the blood trail. These marks can be subtle or obvious, depending on the age and ability of the group. Each person takes a turn in front, leaving trails and marks indicating the direction in which they are travelling. Once everyone has had a turn, or the two minutes are up, the group finds somewhere to hide.

The hunters now begin their hunt. If walkie-talkies are being used, they can communicate that they have started looking and the groups can send gruesome noises to one another. The hunters can then follow the flour trail to find their prey. Again, they must travel in a line, one behind the other. The person at the front is the only one looking for a sign. Each person has a turn, then goes to the back, until the mammoth is found.

Observation stations

This is a great activity for those wanting to test their powers of observation. It challenges your sight and helps strengthen your field of vision.

AGE 5+
TIME 10+ minutes
TOOLS None
MATERIALS Ten or so items of varying sizes and colours, length of string/cord

Using some string or cord, mark out an area in one long line for the participants to stand behind. Place the items you have chosen randomly, reaching out about a maximum of 20 large paces away from your string line. Using all of the area, put some of the items up close and others far away. Loop some of the items over branches, and lean big items up against trees. Match the colour or shape of your items to blend into the background. Make sure that you can still see them when you stand behind the string line. Don't tell the people who will be observing what you've hidden or how many items there are.

Bring your observers to stand behind the string and ask them to spot as many items as they can. They must remain quiet throughout and not signal to others when they see something.

Stalking walks

Imitating animals gives a fascinating insight into how they walk or fly, look, listen and stalk. These activities are great for developing and sharpening your senses (such as sight and hearing) and improving your stealth skills.

Owl eyes

Stand in an area where there is enough space for everybody taking part to stretch out their arms. Stretch them in front of your body and wiggle your fingers. Looking forwards, slowly move your hands out to the sides until they are just out of vision. This should be somewhere in line with your ears.

Stretch out your arms again and, looking forwards, move them up and down until they just go out of sight. You will be amazed at how much you can see. The more you practise with your owl eyes (your peripheral vision), the better you will be at spotting movement – just like a hunter.

Did you know that humans have great eyesight, too? We can see from right in front of our face to just in front of our ears.

Fox walk

Foxes are sneaky scavengers and can move very silently and slowly. This exercise helps you find your inner fox. Stand in an area where there is enough space for everybody taking part to spread out and stand still.

Try taking one single step that takes 30 seconds to complete. Start with the part of the step where your leg takes a stride. Move it forwards as slowly and smoothly as you can. Now practise placing your foot down stealthily: heel down first, then the outside of the foot, then place the whole foot down.

Combine the 30-second step with the stealth foot and move through the open area, going very, very slowly.

Deer listen and leap

Deer have a great sense of smell and amazing hearing – their big, alert ears are always listening out for danger.

To listen like a deer, be completely silent. Once you have heard all the different sounds around you, cup your hands behind your ears. Listen again, and your hearing should be amplified.

Now you are hearing like a deer, leap and jump around like one, too.

Camouflage hands

Camouflage is the art of matching your natural environment, and animals are experts at it. Deer, with their many shades of brown, complement the foliage and trees around them. Frogs, with their green skin, match the lily pads on ponds. See how easy or hard it is to camouflage a part of your body. Younger children can try camouflaging just a finger.

AGE Any
TIME 5+ minutes
TOOLS None
MATERIALS Natural materials such as leaves, mud and moss, water for making mud

Step 1
Choose a tree. Observe its colours, patterns, any knots, etc. Collect materials to match your tree's colours and textures. Make some mud using earth and water.

Step 2
Place your hand on your tree or at the base of it. Using the materials you collected, decorate your hand to match the tree. Continue up your arm for a more ambitious project.

1

Camouflage is not the art of hiding, it is the art of blending in.

2

Get to know a tree

There are many ways in which you can get to know a tree: feel its bark, stand back and admire it, or if possible find out its history and work out its height and age. Below are some ways you can do that – and no, you don't have to chop down a tree to guess its age!

Touch the tree game

In pairs, put a blindfold on one person. The other will lead him or her safely to a tree (guiding by an elbow is advisable). The blindfolded person will feel the tree. Notice where its branches are. Is the bark rough or smooth? Is it a tall tree or stumpy? Does it have leaves that you can touch?

When they have had enough time, they should be led back (by a different way) to the place they started from to take off their blindfold. They then have to guess which tree was theirs. Then swap over.

Trees make a perfect resting spot to have a go at the Sit spot activity on page 15.

Tree facts

A bristlecone pine (*Pinus longaeva*) in the White Mountains, California, is thought to be the oldest tree in the world at nearly 5,000 years old. The tallest tree is thought to be about 380ft (116m) high, a coast redwood (*Sequoia sempervirens*) living in the Redwood National Park in Northern California.

How old is it?

This is a fun way to estimate a tree's age without chopping it down to count its rings. This can only be a rough estimate: each tree grows at a different rate, so there is no foolproof method that works for all trees. Also, we use our hand width as a guide and, just like trees, we are all different and therefore have different sizes of hands. Each hand span equals about five years. See how many hand spans are needed to reach around the trunk of a tree. Add these up in multiples of five to see how old the tree is.

How many people are needed to give your tree a group hug?

How tall is it?

Stand with your back touching the tree you want to measure. Take a few big steps away from it and put your head between your legs to look behind you. Can you see the top of the tree? If not, stand up and take a few more giant steps away. Keep checking the view in between your legs. When you can see the tip of the tree, count your paces back. Each pace should be around 3ft (1m) long. Therefore, if you can measure 20 paces back to the tree, your tree is about 65ft (20m) tall.

Colour chart nature matching

I love the simplicity of this activity. It can be done anywhere, for any length of time, in any weather, with as many or as few people as you like. You are likely to be amazed at how many colours can be seen when you start to look.

AGE Any
TIME Any
TOOLS A colour chart card
MATERIALS None

Most hardware and DIY shops have colour charts available to take home. They will probably have many with variations of one colour on the card. Take a few different ones so that you have plenty of variety.

Now, with your colour charts, head out into a park, forest or other natural place. See what you can find that matches the colours on your chart.

Things to think about:
- What colours do you expect to see in nature?
- Can you find all the colours on your charts?
- Which colours are easy to find?
- Which colours are hard to find?

Night vision

Did you know that we can see in the dark without any high-tech equipment? Try this simple technique next time you find yourself in the dark around the fire. It is a great way to re-train your night-vision abilities, perfect for trying out when camping to find your way back to your tent in the dark.

AGE 5+
TIME 15+ minutes
TOOLS Eye patch (optional)
MATERIALS A campfire at night, in the dark

Unless it's total darkness around you, this won't work, so spend the time while it is light making a fire and collecting wood. Once it is dark, cover one eye with a hand or close one eye. It's really hard not to peek, so wearing an eye patch is handy, and a great excuse to look like a pirate.

With your open eye, stare into the fire for 15 minutes. Chat to a friend, look for faces in the fire – anything to distract you from the time – but do not look away. When the time is up, look away from the fire and cover the eye that has been open, while opening up the eye that has been closed. Stare into the darkness. You'll be amazed at how clearly you can see, even with just one eye. It's suddenly like you're wearing invisible night-vision glasses. It doesn't last forever, but it will be long enough to know what it is like to see in the dark.

Night walk

Have you ever gone out at night just to find out what you can see and hear? Maybe you've heard a bark or a snuffle, or perhaps a hoot? Venture out and investigate the noises and sights of the night for yourself but, before you go, pack a bag with useful kit to make sure you are equipped for your adventure. Then wait for dusk to fall.

AGE 7+ (with adult supervision)
TIME Any (but I would recommend 1 hour+)
TOOLS See box below of things to take

Things to take with you
- Head torch
- High visibility jacket
- Warm, weatherproof clothing and boots
- Fully charged mobile phone with stored emergency numbers
- Bag
- Camera
- Pair of binoculars
- Notebook

Staying safe

Always make sure you take a responsible adult with you. Have a look at your route and any potential hazards either on the way or at your site. Make sure someone else knows where you are going, how you are getting there and back and what you plan to do when you are there.

Did you know that deer can bark and foxes can make a sound like a cough?

Things you might see and hear

Hedgehogs
Hedgehogs like to hide under garden sheds, near compost heaps or in hedges. You may hear them snuffling and huffing around as they search for food.

Bats
Bats are easiest to spot in the summer months when they are out hunting insects. They particularly like to be by water.

Foxes
Most foxes are shy and secretive, best seen at dusk. Cemeteries and parks can be great places to see them but they can also be seen in towns, busily foraging out in the streets.

Badgers
Go out at dusk to see badgers, but think about the sound your clothing makes when you move. Don't use soap or anything perfumed either. They will sense danger and leave immediately. The best time to look for them is during early to mid-summer.

Owls
Wear dark, quiet clothing. Keep your distance from a nest or roost sites. It's best to arrive at your watching site before dark and remain hidden.

The Moon and stars
It is easy to study the Moon with a pair of binoculars if you stay away from other light sources and make sure you have a clear line of sight, with no trees in the way. The stars you can see will depend on the amount of light pollution in the area.

Try a dawn walk
Head out early, just before the sun rises, and see for yourself who has been prowling, flying or snuffling about – they might still be around. Plus, you'll get to witness first-hand the beautiful dawn chorus of birds as they all start to sing and greet the sun with joy. Follow all of the same safety precautions that you would for a night walk.

OUTDOOR CRAFTS

Whatever the time of the year, nature has an abundance of things you can use to sculpt, mould, stick, collage and make beautiful artwork. The beauty of most nature crafts is that they need few resources or planning and some go straight back into the earth to be composted. When you have completed your activity, don't forget to take a photo, as the wind or rain may reclaim your art.

Nest building

Have you seen how birds build their nests? Isn't it clever? With no teaching, they instinctively know how to build a nest using just their beaks. Could you do that? Try using some of the materials they do to weave a solid nest. Use grasses, bits of fluff, sticks, feathers, leaves, mud and more.

AGE Any
TIME 10+ minutes
TOOLS None
MATERIALS Any natural materials you can find, like grass, sticks, feathers and mud

To begin, take a rough bundle of grass, make a loop and then weave in the ends to create your nest-like shape. Start small and keep adding materials, threading more materials in, weaving long grasses through. Then just keep adding. See how long it takes you to get something that resembles a bird's nest. It might be harder than you think!

Birds can collect all the material and build a nest using only their beaks!

Bird feeder

This is a great activity for the winter months when food stores for birds are depleted. They will appreciate extra help in getting their food so they can survive through this cold season.

AGE Any
TIME 10+ minutes
TOOLS Scissors
MATERIALS
Lard, bird seed, pine cones, string, bowl. Plastic gloves and aprons are all advisable

Step 1
Gather as many pine cones as you want to make bird feeders. Mix together the lard and bird seed in a bowl and squish them together with your hands.

Step 2
Tie the string to the top of the pine cone, leaving a long tail to tie it onto a tree or bird-feeding station.

Step 3
Squash the mixture around the pine cone, making sure it sinks into all the nooks and crannies. Tie the cone to a tree and wait patiently until the birds begin to trust their gift from you.

Using a pine cone as a base means the lard sticks better and the bird feeder will hold together for longer.

1

2

3

Goblin village and mini dens

Start this activity with the story below, which describes why there are no longer goblins around here – their village was destroyed by a clumsy dragon. Then set to work rebuilding the lost village, with theme park, gardens and bridges galore!

AGE 3–6 years
TIME 15+ minutes
TOOLS None
MATERIALS Natural materials such as moss, sticks, leaves and stones

The story of the goblin village (for inspiration)

Have you ever seen a goblin? No? Well, that's because they no longer come here. Here, where we stand, there used to be the most amazing goblin village. It had houses that were joined by epic bridges and gardens that looked like theme parks. It had cinemas, sweet shops and dance halls where goblins would meet up. A very friendly, large dragon, who lived up the hill, heard about these dances. He loved dancing and desperately wanted to join in the fun.

One particularly rainy day, he put on his dancing shoes and ran down from the top of the valley to find the dance hall. But the rain had turned the ground into mud so he slipped all the way down. He slipped past all the trees, through the forest, down the hill and landed in a heap, squashing the whole village. Not one building was left standing. The goblins had no choice but to leave, and now no one knows where they live. It's terribly sad. I wish there was some way we could help . . .

Once you have read the story, decide what to build. A post office, a house, a park? Find places that have interesting characteristics: a hole at the bottom of a tree, creeping roots, low overhanging branches and so on. Use natural materials to create tiny dens. Add leaves on sticks for miniature trees, pebbles lined up as bridges, moss for roofs and more. You can use small teddies or other toys as a guide for size.

3D maps

This can be a craft activity or part of a fun game. It's great for encouraging creativity, getting to know the area you are in and understanding the features of the surrounding environment.

AGE 3+
TIME 10+ minutes
TOOLS None
MATERIALS Whatever can be found on the ground: stones, twigs, leaves, etc

As a group, or individually, walk around the area. Notice the main features: trees that stand out; a hedge line; different sizes of trees and plants; is there a stream, path or gate? Decide on names for the features that stick out the most, for example, 'the wise old oak tree'; 'the wiggly jiggly path' or 'the happy family of trees'.

Mark out an area about 3 x 3ft (1 x 1m) using logs or sticks around the edge. Use whatever natural materials you can find around you to create a 3D map of the area within this log frame. Once it is finished, share the scene with others, talking them through the map, explaining the key features and what they are called.

3D map game

To play this as a game, you will need two or more players. Each person will make their own map but not talk anyone through its features when they have finished. One player will hide a clothes peg somewhere in the surrounding area without the other player(s) seeing. He or she will then come back and place a peg in the corresponding area of the map. The other player(s) then have to find the hidden peg based on its location on the map, trying to decipher what all the sticks, stones, pine cones, etc symbolize.

Playing with clay

Clay is nature's answer to play dough – there is so much messy fun to be had. Source your own natural clay following the instructions below or, if you prefer, you can use air-dry clay instead. Grab a ball and then simply let your imagination run wild.

The creatures you decide to make may only exist in your imagination.

Natural clay

Natural clay can be found near riverbeds; look out for milky-looking water. It has a distinctive, slippery feel and can be red, orange, grey and even white. Collect what you need and mix it with water until it is thin enough to be filtered out, then pour the mixture through a sieve or muslin cloth. Leave the watery mixture for a day or two so the clean clay settles at the bottom. Pour off the top layer and dry the clay out a bit more before using.

If you leave your creations out in the rain, they will turn back into sloppy clay.

Clay bugs

Grab a ball of clay. Press leaves in to make wings; push sticks in to make legs and antennae; find acorn shells or seeds to make eyes, and so on. Leave the clay to dry.

Trolls, elves and goblins

Roll a small ball of clay for the head and a larger ball for the body. Attach them together with a small stick. Insert more sticks into the body to make the legs and arms. Add seed eyes, moss hair, a leaf beard and whatever else your troll desires. Leave the troll to dry.

Clay tree spirits

Find an interesting tree. It could be big or small, old or young, thick or thin. Press a big dollop of clay (or sticky mud) onto the tree. This will be its face. Use this as a base into which you can mould or press natural materials to create features. Give your tree a moustache from long grasses, beady eyes with acorn shells, hair with moss, and so on.

Hedgehogs

Make an oval body with a pointy head from one piece of clay. Cover it in tiny sticks for prickles and add four sticks at the bottom to make legs. Leave the clay to dry.

Leaf printing

An alternative to bark rubbing, this is a great way to transfer the patterns and colours of nature's plants onto fabric. You could use these beautiful pieces of art as part of another project. Tie them onto a stick to make a wall hanging or tapestry or sew a few of them together to make a nature collector's bag.

AGE Any
TIME 5+ minutes
TOOLS Chopping board (or any hard surface), scissors, hammer, mallet or pounding stone
MATERIALS Cotton sheet, common abundant plants

Step 1
Cut out a square from the cotton sheet to the size you want.

Step 2
Collect the plants you want to use in your design. Bracken, buttercups, dock leaves and tree leaves all work well. Be sure you don't pick anything poisonous: if in doubt, leave it out. Only use fresh plants and flowers and only pick from areas where the plants are abundant.

This activity works best in spring and summer when the leaves and plants are full of moisture.

Step 3
Place the plants either one at a time or in a pattern on the chopping board or hard surface. Put the cotton square over the top. Using the hammer or mallet, repeatedly hit the area where the plants are underneath.

Step 4
Watch as a colourful pattern comes through the fabric.

3

4

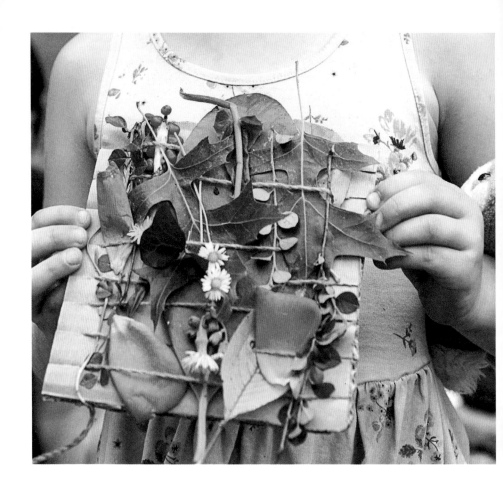

Nature weaving

Weaving is a great way to explore the textures and colours found in nature. It offers a way to make art, have some quiet time and keep little hands busy. One of the things I love about this activity is that it is easy enough for pre-schoolers but older children will enjoy it too. The older they are, the more advanced and intricate the weave can be. The finished masterpieces look great hanging up in the house or even displayed outside.

AGE 3+
TIME 30 minutes+
TOOLS Scissors, secateurs
MATERIALS Sticks, plants and herbs from the garden like lavender, or flowers and plants growing in the grass such as daisies, dandelions, plantain, etc. Thick cardboard (a minimum of 6 x 6in/15 x 15cm), yarn or ribbon and tape

1

Step 1

Create the loom to weave the natural materials into. Take some thick cardboard and cut small slits along two opposite edges. They need to be big enough to keep yarn or ribbon in place, about ³/₈in (1cm) deep and ³/₈in (1cm) between each cut.

Step 2

Start at one end and begin wrapping yarn or ribbon round and round the card, tucking it into the slits as you go. Leave a 2in (5cm) tail hanging out to tie off at the end and secure each end with a piece of tape. You are now ready to weave.

Step 3

Gather up materials to weave into your loom such as long grass and flowers. Weave each piece over and under from one end to the other. It's nice to be able to fill your loom but equally as effective with just a few pieces.

2

3

Making a stick loom

Lash four sticks together into a square. Create the strings using yarn secured at the top of the frame and then loop the yarn all the way to the bottom horizontal stick. Continue along the frame until it is filled. Each time you wrap the yarn around either the top or bottom rung you need to do a full turn of the yarn. Weave in your foraged materials as before.

Natural collages and sculptures

Nature provides us with wonderful materials to make art; your imagination is the only limit. These pieces of natural artwork are temporary and will be returned to nature, sometimes even within hours! Take a photo as a reminder.

Making a start

Look around you before you decide what to make. Sometimes the materials will guide you and show you what is possible. Decide whether you want to make a 3D structure that stands proud and tall or a framed picture that sits beautifully on the ground. Gather your materials and create a wonderful picture or sculpture by placing or building them up.

Ideas for sculptures

- Make an abstract piece of art. Art does not always have to look like something we recognize; sometimes it is about making something interesting, beautiful or thought-provoking.

- Make a 3D person or a self-portrait.
- Make a 3D creature: a centipede from a log with a hundred sticks for legs; a snail made from a nest of grass; a bird made with logs, feathers and stones, etc.

Natural collage ideas

- Use the seasons as a guide. Divide your picture into four sections. Think about what you might see or feel during each season and use natural materials to represent this: bright dandelions in summer representing the sun, brown leaves representing autumn, a snowman made from daisies and such like.
- Use natural materials to create a favourite holiday memory, as if your picture were a photograph on the ground.
- Create a picture of yourself or a friend.

Only use materials that can be found in large quantities or are already on the ground.

Leaf bunting

This activity is super simple, yet really effective. The bunting lasts a surprising amount of time when you use fresh leaves. It is also easy enough for really young children to join in. Use to decorate a den or in your house to bring nature indoors.

AGE Any
TIME 20 minutes+
TOOLS Craft hole punch in various shapes (or an office-style circular hole punch will do)
MATERIALS A selection of leaves (fresh and waxy ones like rhododendron work best, but any will work fine), a length of ribbon (depending on how long you want your bunting to be)

Step 1

Go out for a walk and collect your leaves. About ten is a good number. If it's not a tree from your own garden, make sure you are respectful and do not take too many from one tree and ask permission if the tree is on someone's private property. Use your hole punch to make patterns in the leaves.

Step 2

Cut as many shapes into them as you like, but make sure you leave some leaf still connected in between each hole.

Step 3

Thread your leaves onto the ribbon using the holes that you punched. Now hang up the bunting and enjoy.

You could also paint your leaves and, if you place a sheet of paper underneath, you'll make interesting designs under the leaves, too.

Stick boats

This simple activity combines crafts with exploration, and you can make these little sail boats from foraged materials. With just a couple of simple steps, you'll soon be sailing the high seas or at least a few puddles, streams or even your kitchen sink if you want to test them out first!

AGE 2+

TIME 5 minutes+

MATERIALS Foraged materials like bark, leaves, flowers, cocktail sticks, paddling pool/sink/bucket (or stream if you have access), paper straws for racing

From your foraged materials, find yourself a base. A flattish piece of bark or light piece of wood works well. Now find a sail. A leaf works beautifully. Use a cocktail stick to fix the sail onto the base by carefully passing it through the leaf at the top and bottom and then pressing it down into the bark to secure in place. You can also use your imagination to construct your own boat design however you like.

More ideas

- Remember, masts and sails don't necessarily make them go faster in a race: it just means you can see them for longer as they drift away so make them big and bold if you can!
- Can you find enough feathers to make a beautiful sail?
- Try using grass to weave around the base of the boat, or use flowers as sails.
- Try tying up a bundle of sticks to make a buoyant base.

Have a boat race using paper straws to blow wind into the sails to propel them along.

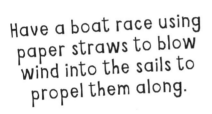

Leaf and flower plaques

These clay plaques look lovely hung up to bring a bit of nature inside your home. Experiment with the flowers and foliage you can find outside to show off the shapes of the natural world. You could even paint them afterwards as a colourful alternative.

AGE 3+
TIME 5+ minutes
TOOLS Rolling pin
MATERIALS Air-dry or natural clay (see page 34), leaves, flowers and sticks. Daisies, dandelions, plantain, ivy and hawthorn leaves are lovely for this.

Step 1
Roll out a fist-sized piece of clay to make a tile shape, about ³/₈in (1cm) thick.

Step 2
Place your chosen leaves and flowers onto the clay tile. Use the rolling pin to roll gently over the plants. Do this a few times to ensure their pattern has transferred onto the clay.

Step 3
Now take away the plants. You should be left with a beautiful indent.

Step 4
You can leave the plaque natural or paint it. If you want to hang it up, make two holes at the top with a stick before the clay dries.

Things to do with conkers

A favourite autumnal activity for many children is to go hunting for horse chestnuts (conkers). The only problem is what to do with the large collection that accumulates at home. We've painted them, painted with them, drawn faces on them, used them in a bowl in a corner to fend off spiders, even made soap with them. Here are some of our favourite ideas.

Conker facts

Found on the horse chestnut tree (*Aesculus hippocastanum*), conkers are NOT edible. Horse chestnut trees have very large hand-shaped leaves, with five to seven leaflets and spiky shells around the nut. Do not confuse horse chestnut with sweet chestnut (*Castanea sativa*), which has single long leaves and the chestnuts can be roasted and eaten.

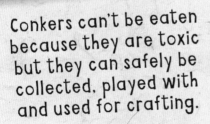

Conkers can't be eaten because they are toxic but they can safely be collected, played with and used for crafting.

Conker games

Draw a cross on some and a circle on others with acrylic paint pens. Make a criss-cross board with sticks and play tic-tac-toe (noughts and crosses).

Conker animals

Make holes for legs, ears, antlers, etc. and press in cocktail sticks. Try to break up lots of cocktail sticks and cover one whole side to make a cute little hedgehog.

Conker art

Lay some paper on a tray. Paint the conkers with thick paint and place onto the paper. Use the tray to roll them around to make colourful designs.

You could make a mini den for your conker creatures to inhabit (see page 32).

Conker spiders

First make eight holes in the conker where you want the legs to be, using a screwdriver or metal skewer. Stick in pipe cleaners as legs. Glue on googly eyes.

Conker caterpillar

Using a screwdriver or metal skewer, make a hole all the way through each conker. About ten is a good number. Using yarn and a blunt needle, thread through the conkers and tie a big knot at the end so that they don't fall off. Glue on googly eyes. Paint a design on the rest of the body.

Conker soap

The seeds (conkers), the leaves and the bark of the horse chestnut tree all contain a very useful compound called saponin. Saponins have incredible cleaning properties and have been used for centuries for their similarities with soap.

To make soap, grate the conkers into a bowl. Pour warm water from the kettle into a glass jar. Add the grated conkers to the warm water and leave it to steep. You can use the mixture after about half an hour, once it has turned milky, but it's even better left overnight. When your soapy mixture is ready, you can use it to wash grubby hands, just like soap. Make sure you rinse them very thoroughly afterwards. You can even put it in the washing machine as a biodegradable laundry soap.

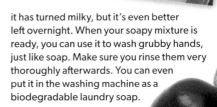

USEFUL KNOTS

Knowing how to tie a range of basic knots is
a very handy bushcraft skill that will help you in
all manner of tasks, from assembling a shelter to
making an emergency stretcher. Here we teach
you some of the most useful knots to know.

Glossary of knot terms

Bight

A bight of rope refers to a bend in the rope.

Hitch

A hitch attaches a rope to something. There are different types of hitch but the most commonly used is a double half hitch (see page 55).

Frapping turn

If you make a lashing, a frapping turn can be used to make it tight. You wrap the rope round and round and then pull the rope tight before tying off.

Working end

The end of the rope you are using to tie the knot.

Standing end

The end of the rope that stays still while tying the knot.

Quick release

A quick release knot is where a bight of rope has been pulled through while tying the knot. This is a safety feature that allows the knot to be untied quickly.

Loop

A loop is made when a rope forms a partial circle with the ends crossing each other.

Slip knot

This is a simple loop on the end of a string or rope that will loosen when the tail is pulled.

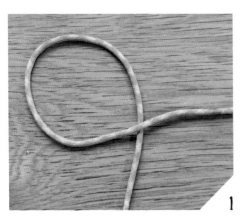

1

2

Step 1
Form a loop at the end of your rope by placing the right-hand side of the rope on top of the left. Pinch the rope where it overlaps with your thumb and forefinger.

Step 2
With your other hand, take the working end of the rope and push a loop through the back of the first loop you formed.

This is a useful temporary knot that is quick to tie and even quicker to undo.

3

Step 3
Pull until tight and the loop is secure. To release, pull the working end and the loop should slip through.

Sheet bend

The sheet bend is a useful knot for tying two ropes together. You can even use two different types and thickness of ropes or string. This is a great knot when you find yourself needing that extra bit of length.

Step 1
Form a bight (bend) in one piece of rope.

Step 2
Pass the new piece of rope through the bight.

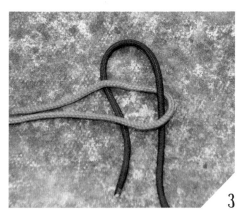

Step 3
Pass it around the back of the first piece of rope.

Step 4
To finish, tuck the new rope under itself and pull tight.

Clove hitch

The clove hitch is useful for starting or finishing a lashing such as a square lashing.

Step 1
Pass the end of the rope around the object you need to secure it to.

Step 2
Cross over the standing end of the rope.

Step 3
Loop the rope back around the object.

Step 4
Thread it back under itself and pull tight.

Double half hitch

More secure than a single hitch, this is mainly used for finishing and tying off.

Step 1
Loop the rope around the object you need to secure it to.

Step 2
Pass the working end up through the loop.

Step 3
Pull the working end tight against an object. Take the working end under the standing rope and pass it back through the loop.

Step 4
Pull the knot tight.

Siberian hitch

This is an excellent knot for making a ridge line for supporting a tent but should not be trusted for bigger loads as it could slip. It can be tied with gloved hands in cold weather and, with its quick release, is easily undone.

Step 1
Pass the rope over your hand and around the back of the tree.

Step 2
Pass the working end under your hand and back over your fingers.

Step 3
Pass the working end over both ropes between your hand and the tree and back under.

Step 4
Tuck a bight (bend) between your fingers.

Step 5
Pull this bight through the loop.

Step 6
Tighten the quick release.

Step 7
Pull the knot tight against the tree.

Step 8
To release, pull the tail.

Timber hitch

The timber hitch knot is great for pulling a log or a stack of sticks. This knot locks when you apply pressure by pulling an object, but practically falls apart when you release the rope.

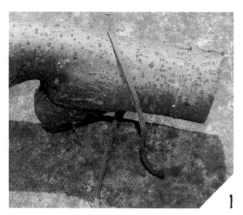

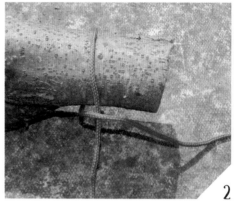

Step 1
Pass the rope around the log.

Step 2
Pass the working end over the standing end (the non-moving piece).

The timber hitch is especially good for putting up a tarpaulin shelter or hammock.

Step 3
Bring the working end up on the log.

You can attach one side to a tree and know that it is secure. It is particularly good as it is self-tightening and easy to undo.

Step 4
Loop the working end around itself once.

Step 5
Loop the working end around itself once more.

Step 6
Repeat for a third time. The friction of the knot will hold it tight.

Prusik

The Prusik is a good knot for holding in place tarps on a tent line, as it locks in place under pressure. It is also easily moveable when pressure is released.

Step 2
Repeat step 1 and pull the knot tight.

Step 1
Form a bight (bend) in the rope and place it over the tent line. Pull the two ends through the bight and wrap around the tent line.

If putting up a larger tarp, you can add in more loops around your tent line to make the Prusik stronger.

Step 3
Attach the ends to your tarp loop and tie a sheet bend (see page 53) on a bight.

Canadian jam knot

This knot uses little rope and is useful for wrapping up and tying down sleeping bags and big loads. It is also known as an arbor knot.

Step 1
Form a loop in the rope. Pass the working end behind and through the loop to form an overhand knot.

Step 2
Repeat step 1 to tie a second overhand knot next to the first.

Step 3
Pass the standing end of the rope around your object and through the first overhand knot.

Step 4
Pull the knots tight against your object.

Slippery guy-line knot

This knot is great for securing tarps and can be adjusted when the cord is taut. It can be undone under load, too. It is also known as a taut line.

Step 1
Bring the rope from your object (tarp) down around your peg to form a loop.

Step 2
Pass the working end through the loop and around the tight line.

Step 3
Repeat step 2 twice. You will have three turns around the rope.

Step 4
Pass the working end behind the ropes leaving a bight (bend) of rope.

FOREST SCHOOL HANDBOOK

5

Step 5
Form a new bight of rope with the working end and pass it through the first bight to form the quick release.

Step 6
Tighten your knot and slide it upwards to tighten and downwards to release the pressure.

6

This knot can also be used to make a handy washing line when you are camping out.

Square lashing

This knot is used to secure poles into a rectangle that can be used for a raft, tabletop and many other bushcraft items.

Step 1
Start by tying a clove hitch (see page 54) on the pole underneath, next to where the two poles form a cross.

Step 2
Wrap the working end over and under the poles alternating either side of the pole underneath. Do this three times, pulling tight as you go.

Step 3
When the wrapping has been done, bring the working end back around between the two logs and wrap three times round, pulling tight as you go. This is called a frapping turn (see page 51).

Step 4
With the working end, tie another clove hitch to finish.

Shear lashing

Use this simple knot to join two poles together.

Step 1
Tie a clove hitch (see page 54) around one pole.

Step 2
Wrap both poles with a simple lashing (weaving the working end in and out between the two poles), going round several times.

Step 3
Wrap the lashings with three frapping turns (see page 51), pulling tight as you go.

Step 4
Tie off the end with another clove hitch.

SHELTERS AND DENS

One of my favourite, and completely free, things to do is to build a shelter or base out of natural materials. The best place for this is in the woods. There you can find most of the materials you will need to construct your den, and there is often no need to cut anything down. We have also included some shelters that use tarps for a really quick and simple build. Of course, you can freestyle your own, but over the following pages are some simple designs to have a go at.

Tarp bender

This shelter makes a great group den or a warm shelter on a wet day. It is very quick and easy to build using a tarp, poles and some string.

AGE 6+

TIME 25+ minutes

TOOLS Folding saw, mallet

MATERIALS Tarp, six hazel poles, about 1in (2.5cm) in diameter and 8ft (2.4m) long, string/paracord, one thicker hazel pole about an arm's length long and 3in (8cm) in diameter, six pegs

KNOTS Canadian jam knot (see page 61) or square lashing (see page 64)

Step 1

Cut six hazel poles 8ft (2.4m) tall and 1in (2.5cm) in diameter. Cut one thicker hazel pole; about an arm's length and 3in (8cm) diameter. This will be used to make post holes.

Step 2

Make two holes in the ground, using the thicker pole, about 6ft (1.8m) apart. Place two of the 8ft (2.4m) hazel poles into one hole. Twist them together and then bend them over to form an arch. Push the opposite ends into the other hole so that the arch stays upright. This arch will form the doorway.

Step 3

Use a stick to draw a large semicircle starting from one side of the doorway, curving around back to the other. This marks where the back of the bender will be and should have a radius of about 5ft (1.5m). Along this line, make four more holes in the ground, spaced about 2ft (60cm) from one another, and place the remaining four hazel poles into them.

Step 4

Allow the natural curve of the poles to bend towards the doorway. Make sure they are secure in the ground, or the shelter will lift up.

Step 5

Bend each pole inwards towards the doorway.

Step 6
Secure them onto the arch with a Canadian jam knot or square lashing.

Step 7
Throw the tarp over the frame and peg it down through the loops at the back to secure it.

This shelter is perfect for sleeping in. With a fire outside you will stay cosy and dry inside.

A-frame shelter

This simple shelter is fun to build for all ages and makes a great team-building challenge. See which team can make the best waterproof A-frame shelter. To make sure it is truly waterproof, test it with a full watering can afterwards!

AGE 4+
TIME 45+ minutes
TOOLS Folding saw, leaf litter bag (optional)
MATERIALS Leaves, wood, grasses, string/paracord
KNOTS Canadian jam knot (see page 61)

Step 1

Find a log that is as tall as you with your arm stretched above your head, and two large sticks with forked ends that reach the tallest person's chest. These will be used to make the doorway.

Make the forked sticks into a triangular shape, leaning them inwards towards one another so that they link and hold together. If you want to guarantee that it will hold, you can tie them together with paracord using a Canadian jam knot. Now place the log on top of the triangle to form the ridge pole. You can tie these all together if you like with another jam knot or some square lashing. These should form a sturdy base for your shelter.

Step 2

Cover both sides with twigs and sticks, making sure to keep enough space inside for a person to lie down. Children often think of this like creating a rib cage. Each stick should have a place; smaller ones down at the bottom, longer ones towards the doorway, like completing a big 3D shelter puzzle. Make sure you leave the doorway free of sticks so that you can get inside, though!

Step 3

Start covering the frame from the ground up, using leaves, twiggy branches and grass. For a well-insulated, waterproof layer you need a thickness of about fingertip to elbow in depth.

If you plan to use your shelter overnight you could throw a tarp over it in case of rain.

Lean-to shelter

This is great for group sleepouts, is simple to construct and can be used effectively with a fire outside as it is open on one side. However, it can be time-consuming to complete the final leaf layer and can cause great disruption to the minibeasts' habitats.

AGE 4+
TIME 45+ minutes
TOOLS Garden sack (optional)
MATERIALS Long poles and sticks, leaves, wood, grasses, string/paracord
KNOTS Timber hitch (see page 58), Canadian jam knot (see page 61), square lashing (see page 64)

1

Step 1

The basic structure is in the shape of a football goal. Find two trees that are far enough apart to fit one person lying down between them. Look for a pole long enough to extend past both trees. Secure the pole to the trees using a Canadian jam knot or a timber hitch. This will be your ridge pole. Make sure the wood is not rotten, as this would make the whole structure weak. This pole needs to sit somewhere between belly button and shoulder height. The lower down the pole, the cosier your den will be, but the more difficult to get in and out of.

2

Step 2

Ask the tallest person to lie down perpendicular to the ridge pole with their head under it. Using a stick, mark out a line where their feet reach. This will show how big you need to make the den. Lay sticks up against the ridge pole, closely together, reaching out to this line. Fill in the sides with sticks, too.

3

Step 3

Once you have finished
laying all the poles in place,
cover the area in twigs. This
will help to stop the leaves
falling through.

Step 4

Now insulate and
waterproof the shelter by
adding a thick layer of dried
leaves, twiggy branches,
grasses or whatever the
woodland floor may offer.
Ideally, this layer will
reach a depth of fingertip
to elbow to be properly
effective as a survival den.
But if you're only spending
one night in it, or just
enjoying a day's play,
simply cover it in dead
leaves or grasses – just
enough to fill in the gaps.
If you have a garden sack,
fill it with leaves and pour
them over your den.

4

If you're going to spend
a night out in your new
home, why not try a long
log fire (see page 86) to
help keep you warm?

Baker's tarp

A tarp is a simple and quick way to make a shelter that doesn't destroy the local minibeasts' habitats. There are many tarps designed for camping; we use one with 19 points, which can give you many configurations for shelters. We offer two different designs of tarp shelters over the next few pages. This one is great for groups to sleep under on long, summer nights.

AGE 4+

TIME 10+ minutes

TOOLS Mallet

MATERIALS Tarp 10 x 10ft (3 x 3m), enough rope/cord to fit between two trees (about 30ft/10m), pegs, two sticks 3ft (1m) long, 12ft (4m) of paracord

KNOTS Siberian hitch (see page 56), double half hitch (see page 55), Prusik (see page 60), clove hitch (see page 54), slippery guy-line knot (see page 62)

Step 1

Find two trees about 15ft (5m) apart, lay out the rope and tie a Siberian hitch around one of the trees.

Step 2

Feed the rope through the second row of loops on the tarp lengthways (about a third along). Wrap the rope around the other tree and tie a double half hitch with a bight (quick release).

Step 3

Tie a Prusik knot on each side of the tarp attached to the tent line to secure it in place.

Step 4

Peg down the rear two corners of the longest side of the tarp to form the back of the shelter.

Step 5

With a length of rope, tie a double half hitch to the tarp loop on the front corner of each side.

Step 6

With the same piece of rope, now attached to the tarp, leave a short gap and then tie a clove hitch around one of the 3ft (1m) sticks. Repeat on the other side. These sticks will sit on the ground at the front of the shelter. The tension of the pegged-down rope will secure them.

Step 7

With the rope still tied to the stick, bring it to the ground at about a 45-degree angle. Push a peg into the ground and tie a slippery guy-line knot around it with the working end of the rope and tighten. Repeat on the opposite front corner.

A big pile of leaves or ferns are perfect for sleeping on top of. You will stay much warmer by stopping precious body heat from escaping into the cold ground.

FIRE

Fire is an essential part of bushcraft if you
are intending to camp out for any length of time.
It will provide warmth and a means to cook food.
Learning to light a fire is a core outdoor skill that
teaches perseverance as well as science.
It is also very satisfying to achieve success.
The best way to ensure a great fire is to prepare
well. Make sure you have gathered enough
materials to light your fire first.

Fire safety

Always follow these important rules when lighting fires.

- Seek permission from the landowner first.

- Select a safe fire site. Look up and around. Check that your fire is not at the base of any tree, and far away from any roots or overhanging branches.

- Make sure you have a way to extinguish your fire before you begin, such as a bucket of water or a fire extinguisher.

- You can create an obvious area around your fire by placing large logs in a circle around it to prevent children getting too close. Clearly state that they cannot go inside this circle.

Three ingredients of fire lighting

Fire is like a triangle with equal sides. Each side represents an essential ingredient in fire lighting. Each ingredient must be kept in proportion with the others. Too much fuel will suffocate your flames and put it out. Too much air will blow out the fire. Too much heat will burn it out, while too little will not burn at all.

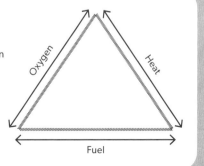

Sources of tinder

Tinder is the first material that the flame or spark will contact, therefore it must be absolutely dry and burn immediately. The best way to use many of these natural tinders is to make a tight nest onto which you then drop an ember (see Lighting a fire using a fire steel, page 82).

Bark

This material can burn very hot but may not be easy to get going. Rough it up using the back of a knife or rock to produce fine sawdust, then light it with a spark from the fire steel. Only use bark from dead fallen trees – there is no need to peel bark from a living tree.

Honeysuckle is a woody vine that can be found in lots of woodlands. When harvesting the bark, remove only the outer layers, which offers itself up naturally; the fibres are long and papery. Prepare the fibre by making two fists, hold the fibres in both hands and rotate the hands forwards. The fibres will break down as they are rubbed together, giving a finer fuel. This is also the favourite building material of field mice, so only take a little.

Dead bracken

Dead and dried bracken can be used to make a tinder bundle if compacted like a small bird's nest.

Fluff or lint

Fluff or lint (from your pockets or clothes dryer) can be used as tinder and is pretty easy to forage.

On a wet day, add a little petroleum jelly to the underside of your cotton wool to give your fire a chance to burn longer.

Seedheads

Cattails grow in ponds and lakes. Their very fluffy seedheads are great to use for extending your coal and can be used in combination with other tinders to produce a sustainable flame. Clematis seedheads also make a great tinder.

King Alfred's cakes

These are rounded black fungi that grow mainly on fallen ash trees. When dried, they act like little coals, taking a spark from your fire steel. They burn slowly, much like a charcoal briquette, with pungent smoke. Fragments can be broken off to expose more embers and be transferred to a tinder bundle to create an open flame.

Cotton wool balls

Shop-bought cotton wool balls are one of my favourite types of tinder to use. They take a spark quickly and easily, igniting into flames. No nest is required.

Char cloth

This is simply cotton or silk scorched black in a tin on a fire (see page 92 to make your own). This is a great tinder and was widely used historically. A spark dropped onto a piece of char cloth will produce an ember, not a flame, until added to a dry tinder nest.

Lighting a fire using a fire steel

A fire steel is a ferrocerium rod that gives off extremely hot sparks (up to 5430°F/3000°C) when it is scraped against a hard, rough surface (usually a piece of steel attached to the rod). Unlike matches or a lighter, fire steels can be used in the wet and claim to have about 12,000 strikes in them.

AGE 5+
TIME 10+ minutes
TOOLS None, but a saw could be handy if you need to cut the wood to size
MATERIALS Fire steel, tinder, dry wood, fire bowl (optional)

Step 1

Find a place to light your fire that follows the safety advice on page 79. Collect dry tinder. This is flammable material that will take a spark easily, such as cotton wool, birch or cherry bark. (See page 80 for a guide on the best tinder to use.)

Step 2

Build a small platform for the fire to sit on. If you sat straight on the ground after rainfall you'd get a wet and cold bottom, with all of your heat escaping into the ground; it's the same for fire. Just a line of dry sticks will do. You could also use a metal fire bowl, which doesn't scorch the ground and leaves no trace.

Step 3

Collect large bundles of three different sizes of dry wood:

1) As thin as a matchstick and as long as your arm.
2) As thin as your finger and as long as your arm.
3) As thick as your wrist and as long as your arm.

3

4

Step 4

A fire steel can be sourced from outdoor shops and online. To use a fire steel, place the striker flat on the top of the ferrocerium rod and use your strength to firmly push them together. Now, still holding that pressure, lift the striker to a 45° angle. Keeping the pressure and angle steady, scrape all the way down with your rod, pinning down the cotton wool to ignite a spark. If you find it difficult to maintain the pressure, start with the striker halfway down the rod. While a fire steel is a great way to start a fire, matches may be appropriate when you don't want to disturb your fire lay. Strike a spark onto your tinder.

If your fire is struggling, you can gently lift a bundle of sticks to encourage oxygen to the core of your fire. This should instantly create more flames.

5

Step 5

When the tinder is alight, carefully put on a large bundle of '1s'. Remember – too little and your fire will not take. Lay the 1s carefully on top of your flame. Once you hear a gentle crackle, the fire is starting to take. Lay on another bundle of 1s, holding them carefully at one end. Gently lay these on in a criss-cross fashion, like a waffle or a Jenga stack.

Step 6

Continue layering up the wood like this. Once you have used all the 1s, start adding the 2s in the same way, then gradually add your 3s, always considering the fire triangle (see page 79). Lay your 3s to create the fire according to your needs, whether that is warmth or cooking, and considering the weather.

6

Fire lays

Whether it is for tea making, cooking, light, a hearth to gather around or to keep myself and a group warm, I never spend a day out in the woods without lighting a fire. How I build that fire depends on what I need to use it for. Below is a guide that will help you decide.

Tipi fire

Use
This is not good for cooking, as it doesn't create a substantial bed of coals and is not flat, but is effective in creating heat for a group to sit around.

How to make
Place a stick upright in the ground. Pack your tinder loosely around this stick. Lay some kindling against the stick at an angle to form a tipi. Keep one side slightly open so that you can light your tinder. Keep leaning sticks up around the core. Light the tinder. The tipi will enable the fire to burn upwards, allowing good draught. Add in the other fuel as the fire gets established.

Criss-cross/upside-down fire

Use
Good for producing coals for cooking.

How to make
This fire breaks the rule of using thin-to-thick materials that start from the bottom; this fire is constructed with the bigger logs at the bottom with kindling and tinder placed above. When the tinder is lit, gravity takes hold and the fire and embers fall onto the fuel below, igniting each consecutive layer as it grows.

Star fire

Use

This is a great fire if you are leaving base camp for some time and want your fire to continue to hold heat and smoulder until you return. The logs are fed in lengthways and then drawn apart to leave glowing embers and ash (for cooking) in the centre. It is very useful for conserving fuel. It produces little flame or smoke when required and can be easily stoked by pushing the logs inwards occasionally.

How to make

A star fire is formed by making a small fire and arranging logs around the outside facing inwards to form the points of a star. To start the fire going strong again, simply push the logs together and blow to add a little oxygen. The long sticks should work as insulation to keep your coals ignited.

Long log fire

Use

This fire is especially good for using in conjunction with natural shelters. If built efficiently and used with a fire reflector, you can keep warm even without a sleeping bag in cold conditions.

How to make

Make three or so small fires in a line. When they are burning well, you can start to extend the length by adding additional longer logs and placing them horizontally. The long fire works well on cold nights when you need continuous warmth. Ideally you need logs as long as your body to provide maximum warmth. These will burn long and slow and require minimal work once established.

V-shaped fire

Use

This fire provides good coals for cooking and can easily sustain itself given the right amount of wood. This method works especially well in windy conditions. Often the wind can cause problems, but this method uses the wind to help the fire.

How to make

Collect large bundles of kindling as long as your arm from fingertip to elbow at least. Separate your kindling into four good handfuls. Think about which way the wind is blowing. Even if there is only a slight breeze, take note. Kneel with your back to the wind and place your handfuls of kindling in a V-shape with the open side of the V facing you, overlapping one another at the tip.

Place your chosen tinder just under the tip of your triangle and light your tinder. I recommend using a match so as not to disturb your sticks. Keeping the kindling long allows you to adjust the fire as it becomes established. If your fire needs more oxygen, lift the uppermost bundle a little to allow more air into the fire. Layer up dry finger-thick sticks as the fire becomes established.

Using matches

A matchstick can break easily, so when you strike it, apply pressure along its length, not across it. As you strike the match, support the head. Don't be afraid of burning your finger, just remove it at the end of the strike.

On igniting the match, take it straight into cupped hands to protect the flame. Once the match is burning, carefully take the flame to the tinder. Do not drop the matchbox and try to avoid it getting wet.

Firewood

All wood burns differently, at different temperatures and speeds. Knowing what wood to choose will help you make an efficient fire. However, as dried or dead wood is best, sometimes nature decides which wood to burn.

Ash

This is one of the best woods for burning. It will produce a steady flame and good heat output. It can be burnt when green but, like all woods, burns best when dry.

Beech

This produces a steady flame and a good amount of heat, but burns away quickly.

The best woods for campfires are ash, fir, apple, hazel and holly.

Use this poem to help you

These hardwoods burn
well and slowly –
Ash, beech, hawthorn,
oak and holly;

Softwoods flare up
quickly and fine,
Birch, fir, hazel, larch and pine;

Elm and willow you'll regret,
chestnut green and sycamore wet.

Celia Congreve, 1930

Hawthorn

This is a good traditional firewood that has a slow burn with good heat output. We have found it to be one of the hottest and therefore great in pizza ovens. We attempted to cook bread in the coals of a hawthorn fire recently, but due to the high level of heat in the coals alone, our bread burnt within minutes.

Larch

Larch produces a reasonable heat output, but needs to be well seasoned. It burns fast and gives good light.

The best woods for cooking fires are oak, beech, maple, birch and sycamore.

It is especially good to use as a starter wood (for kindling) due to its high content of volatile oils.

Poplar

This is a very smoky wood with a poor burn.

Willow

This is a poor firewood that does not burn well even when seasoned, although it is great as a bow drill wood.

Oak

Oak burns long and slow and is very hot. It can be hard to light, but when it gets going it provides an even heat. It is ideal wood for cooking, as it produces little smoke, which makes cooking on a fire pleasurable, and it adds a lovely smoky flavour to some meats and fishes.

Pine

Pine burns with a good flame and produces good heat when seasoned well. It is relatively easy to process, although can be difficult to split due to all the knots.

Making charcoal

Charcoal has been used since earliest times for many purposes, including as an art material, as fuel and as medicine. It can be used to filter water, to treat sickness, as a pigment, for heating our houses and for cooking delicious barbecue foods, to name just a few of its uses.

AGE 7+
TIME 30 minutes
TOOLS Secateurs, tool to punch a small hole in the tin lid (nail or screwdriver), small plug to fit inside the hole (a stick will work), tongs or heatproof gloves
MATERIALS Small sticks of hazel or willow about pencil thickness, large biscuit tin (for a smaller batch you could use a golden syrup tin, or similar).

What is charcoal?

There is archaeological evidence of charcoal production going back about 30,000 years. Charcoal is mostly pure carbon, called char, made by cooking wood in a low-oxygen environment, and burning off volatile compounds such as water, methane, hydrogen and tar.

Step 1

Light a fire (see page 82). You want a nice bed of coals to work with so the criss cross/upside-down fire (see page 85) would work best. Cut up your sticks. The length will depend on the depth and width of your tin. Cut them to fit inside your tin with the lid on.

Step 2
Punch a hole in the top of your tin to allow the air to escape.

Step 3
Place your sticks inside your tin and nestle it into the coals. The smoke should come out from the hole in a steady stream.

Step 4
Once the smoke stops billowing out, your charcoal should be ready. Using your tongs or heatproof gloves, take the tin off the fire. Immediately plug up the hole – otherwise you risk the material inside combusting when it comes into contact with the oxygen in the air.

Step 5
Leave to cool for 15–20 minutes. See if you can draw a picture with your charcoal. You can practise drawing on rocks for a really authentic-looking picture.

Making char cloth

Char cloth makes an excellent tinder. It is very easy to make using 100% cotton material that has been starved of oxygen and had all of its moisture removed through charring. Char cloth ignites with even the smallest spark and holds a very hot ember. It is commonly used with a flint and steel or ferrocerium rod.

AGE 7+

TIME 30 minutes

TOOLS Scissors, tool to punch a small hole in the tin lid (nail or screwdriver), small plug to fit inside the hole (a stick will work), tongs or heatproof gloves

MATERIALS 100% cotton cloth (such as a tea towel, T-shirt, handkerchief or bandana), large biscuit tin (for a smaller batch you could use a golden syrup tin, or similar)

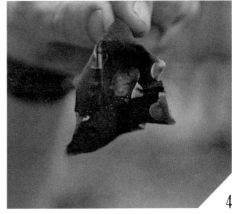

Char cloth is made in the same way as charcoal (see page 90), putting the cloth into an almost airtight tin with a small hole in it, and cooking it in campfire coals until the cloth is completely charred.

Step 1
Light a fire. You need a nice bed of coals to work with. Cut your fabric into small squares about 1½ x 1½in (4 x 4cm).

Step 2
Place the cut-up fabric inside the tin and nestle it into the coals. The smoke should come out from the hole in a steady stream.

Step 3
Once the smoke stops billowing out, the char cloth should be ready. Using tongs or heatproof gloves, take the tin off the fire. Immediately plug the hole, otherwise the material inside may combust when it comes into contact with the oxygen in the air.

Step 4
Leave to cool for 15–20 minutes. Drop a spark onto your cloth and then add to dry tinder to give your fire a great start.

Group bow drill

This is best set up by an adult, but it makes a great group activity with children. Rubbing sticks together to create fire is magical and never fails to get people excited.

AGE 7+
TIME 1 hour+
TOOLS Saw, knife
MATERIALS Firewood (deadwood from willow, sycamore, lime, cedar or poplar), green wood for the bearing block/palm stone, tinder, approx. 30ft (10m) length of rope

Step 1
Saw a piece of deadwood (see materials list) into a plank 1in thick, 12in long and 5in wide (2.5 x 30 x 12.5cm). This will be the hearth.

Step 2
Also using the deadwood, carve a spindle about 15in (38cm) long and about 1in (2.5cm) in diameter and straight.

Step 3
Make the bearing block/palm stone from green wood, about 1ft (30cm) long. Carve out a dip in the middle with a knife.

You can use this method to start a campfire. See pages 83-84, starting at step 5, with your lit tinder bundle.

Step 4

At one end of the hearth and about 1in (2.5cm) in from the edge, carve out a dip for the rounded end of the spindle to fit in. The spindle will be rotated back and forth in it.

Step 5

Cut out a V-shaped notch in the hearth to the edge next to the dip you carved. This can be done either with your knife or a saw.

Step 6

Split the group up so that some are kneeling either side of the hearth. Place the rounded end of the spindle into the dip in the hearth and push down onto the pointed end with the bearing block, nestling it into the carved dip. Wrap the rope around the middle of the spindle and have the group pull back and forth until the notch is filled up with charred wood dust.

Once the notch is filled, speed up the pulling for 10 seconds. If a continuous rising of smoke is seen from the notch, let the ember sit there for about 10-30 seconds to let it grow. Carefully tip the ember into a tinder bundle and then gently blow on it to make flames.

Carrying fire

Most of us do not consider ourselves reliant on fire but our Stone Age ancestors had a different bond with it. They relied on it for survival, for warmth, for protection, for light and for making food more digestible and water safer to drink. Our ancestors may have simply used a large smouldering fungus such as King Alfred's cake or dried birch polypore carried with raw hide cordage.

AGE 9+
TOOLS Tongs or shovel
MATERIALS Bark, dried grasses and leaves, or dried fungus such as King Alfred's cake, an ember, damp cordage or string

Step 1

Collect a combination of some semi-dry grass and leaves and a piece of flexible bark: birch, cedar, etc.

Step 2

Using tongs or a shovel, place a hot coal from your fire directly in the middle of the bark and carefully roll it up tightly around the grass and leaves as if you're making ember sushi. (You can also use a burning King Alfred's cake instead of an ember.)

Step 3

Wrap and tie it as tightly together as possible with some type of cordage, vine, thin green withy or even moistened string or jute.

Step 4

Wait until the bundle begins to smoke and smoulder then pack the ends with moss and dried leaves, etc. The bundle must be tight so that it does not get too much oxygen. Too much oxygen will cause it to burn too fast. Occasionally check it to make sure that it is still smouldering. If you need to, waft it in the breeze, swinging it back and forth to allow oxygen back to the coal. Depending on the size of your original coal your bundle could stay smouldering for 5-8 hours if nurtured correctly.

Step 5

Untie the bundle and blow into it to get the flames of your new fire going.

On days when there was rain or a lack of wood available, the ancient skill of making a tinder bundle to carry an ember would have been vital.

WATER

It's easy to find water in streams, rivers, lakes and puddles. But can we drink it? Many people will say 'no, it's dirty!' Or 'no, it's got germs in!' That's true of untreated water, but you could collect water from any of these sources and drink it if it is filtered and purified correctly. So how do we find, collect and make water safe to drink? This section teaches you some handy tricks.

Collecting water

There are many simple ways to collect water – in a bucket, cup, mess tin or any other receptacle that can hold a liquid. It's fun to see how many ways you can find to collect water.

Rainwater collection

Find four stakes about 3ft (1m) long to place in the ground and tie each corner of your tarp to the stakes. Wait for the rain! Rainwater is only as clean as the vessel that you collect it in, so make sure the tarp is clean as well as the container you use to scoop the water out.

Collecting dew

If you're out camping and wake up early the ground can sometimes be wet with dew. This is fresh water ready to be collected.

Find some long grass. Tie a tea towel or sponges around each of your legs below the knee and walk slowly through the grass. Squeeze out the collected water. You can turn this into a game and see who can collect the most water. Again, remember that the water you collect is only as clean as the vessel you collect it in.

Birch tapping

Another way to find drinkable liquid is to tap sap from a tree. Sap is delicious, with a slightly sweet taste, and can be drunk straight away. Birch trees (Betula species) are the best option, but other possibilities are sycamore (Acer pseudoplatanus) and lime/linden (Tilia).

AGE 4+
TIME 6–24 hours
TOOLS Secateurs
MATERIALS Plastic bottles, string

Step 1

Find a birch tree that is about 15in (35cm) in diameter with branches that can be reached when standing. With the secateurs, snip the end off a small branch and see if it starts to drip with sap. (This branch will heal over by itself in time.)

Step 2

Tie the bottle to the branch and weigh it down so the bottle is as horizontal as possible. Come back in a few hours to see how much sap has been collected. It is best to leave it overnight if possible.

Making birch syrup

You can turn this sap into a syrup: 17 pints (10 litres) of sap makes about 1¾ pints (1 litre) of syrup. To do this, simply boil it down until it thickens. You can even boil it down further to turn it into sugar. The syrup can be used in cooking for both sweet and savoury dishes.

Bottle filter

This filter works well with many layers, taking out the big particles of dirt. It won't remove chemicals or bacteria, however: you will need to kill the bacteria by boiling the water. The combination of filtering and boiling the water makes it safe to drink.

AGE 6+
TIME 20 minutes
TOOLS Scissors
MATERIALS Plastic bottles, piece of cloth, crushed charcoal, gravel, grass, leaves, wood shavings, pine cones (you do not need all the materials listed here, just a combination of small and some large materials so that different layers can be added)

Step 1
Gather all the materials you will need.

Step 2
Cut the bottom off the plastic bottle and remove the lid. Wedge the cloth into the neck of the bottle, then fill it with layers in this order: charcoal, gravel, grass and leaves, wood shavings, pine cones. Make sure everything is compacted down tightly. It is important to keep the layers in this order: the large particles in the water will be filtered out first through the pine cones, while the final layers of crushed charcoal will remove the smaller bits of debris and clean the water.

Step 3
Pour your muddy water slowly through the filter. Be careful not to spill it over the edges, as this will contaminate your clean water. Pass it through the filter several times. If you want to use this water for drinking, you will need to heat it to a rolling boil to kill any potentially harmful germs.

CAMP CRAFT

Camp craft refers to any skills or practice that you may need while camping and is to improve and enhance your time spent outdoors. It is all about knowing how to live comfortably and confidently outside. Your camp should be a place where you feel comfortable, even when far off the beaten track. It is a place where you can rest, plan and prepare for future activities.

Making cordage

Making cordage from natural materials is very simple. There are many materials you can use to create strong cordage, which is used for securing shelters, bow strings, bow-drill fire making, fishing line, tying up a tarpaulin and weaving pots, to name a few. In this example, we are using stinging nettles (Urtica dioica).

AGE 6+

TIME 15 minutes (plus overnight drying)

TOOLS Protective gloves, rock, piece of wood

MATERIALS Nettles

Types of fibre

Here are suggestions for plants that make strong or medium-strength cordage. When harvesting, take only what you need, and pick from many plants rather than from just one area.

Strong fibres
- Stinging nettle
- Lime bark (rotted in water and inner fibres peeled)
- Rosebay willowherb (outer fibres; prepare in a similar way to nettles, gather in winter)
- Sinews
- Horsehair

Medium-strength fibres
- Inner willow bark
- Honeysuckle bark (shedding bark fibres)
- Clematis bark
- Inner elm bark
- Inner sweet chestnut bark

You could use the leaves of the nettles you pick to make the recipes on pages 156–158.

Treating the cordage

When you use material picked in its living form, initially it will have enough food to live for a while, but this will eventually run out and the material will start to break down. Once you have made your cordage, you can add tallow or beeswax to keep it usable, soft and supple. This is somewhat like leather shoes that we need to wax and polish to 'feed' the leather and stop it deteriorating.

Step 1

Harvest the nettles in late summer or early autumn, when they are fully mature or over 3ft (1m) tall. Find a patch of nettles that are tall and straight. With a gloved hand, start from the root and pull the nettle through your gloved hand to strip off the leaves.

Repeat this two or three times to remove the leaves and the fine, hair-like stings.

Step 2

Cut off the roots and tips, place them on a piece of wood and gently break the stalks with a rock.

Step 3

Open out the stalks flat to show the inner bark

Step 4

Bend the stems in half to break the inner bark. Place the outer fibres between your middle finger and index finger and separate them. Do this for about ten nettle strands.

Adding extra fibres

To add extra fibres (splicing), pick three more strands that are equal in size and thickness to the strands already used. Bend them off centre and add them into your existing string with the bend in the V of the fibres. Keep twisting the fibres till you have your desired length.

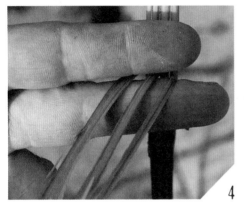

Step 5

Hang the fibres up to dry. When you use them, rehydrate them for 20–30 minutes. Use as many fibres as you wish. Use strands that are equal in thickness for a nice neat string.

Step 6

Find the middle of the length of the fibres. Slightly off the centre point, pinch with both hands then twist in opposite directions to form a loop. While holding the loop, twist the top fibres forwards and bring the bottom fibres over the top. Keep going until you have your required length of cordage.

Giant grass rope

This is one of our favourite activities to do with groups. It shows them that one strand of grass may not be very strong but that many strands brought together can be strong enough to use as a rope swing or even to pull a car!

AGE 4+
TIME 20 minutes
MATERIALS Grass

Step 1
Collect grass that is no shorter than from your fingertips to your elbow; the longer, the better.

Step 2
Lay out two lines of grass opposite each other. When laying the grass, overlap the strands.

Use the rope for a tug of war, to make a rope swing or even a skipping rope.

If the grass has any weak spots, add in more over the weak spot and twist.

3

4

5

Step 3
Divide the group in two and have each side kneel down facing each other on the outside of the grass.

Step 4
Have the team on your left carefully twist the grass clockwise (away from them) and the group on the right twist the grass clockwise (towards themselves). This helps bind the fibres.

Step 5
Once all the grass has been twisted, you can pick up the ends and hold them together firmly. Keep the teams twisting the grass clockwise. As they twist the grass, you turn the ends clockwise. The grass will now be turning into rope. Keep doing this until you get to the end.

Knife safety

Knives are a very important tool in the outdoors and allowing your child to have one is a big step. When the time comes, explain to your child the seriousness and responsibilities that come with having a knife. Mastering knife skills takes time, so practise as often as you can with simple projects.

The different parts of a knife

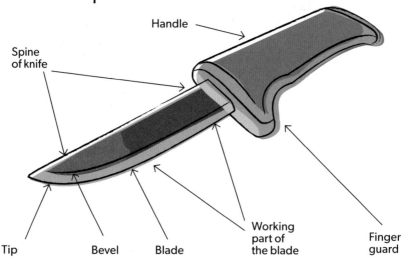

Handle

Spine of knife

Tip

Bevel

Blade

Working part of the blade

Finger guard

Safety checklist

- Always have a good working area on stable ground.
- Try to avoid working with a knife if it is really wet.
- Always carry a first-aid kit with plenty of plasters. Make sure everyone knows where it is kept.
- Make sure everyone knows what the safety bubble is: when sitting, carvers should have no one within an outstretched arm's distance of them, including behind them.
- Always cut away from your body and gripping hand.

- Never move around from your carving spot with an unsheathed knife.
- If you cut yourself, STOP and let someone know, no matter how small the cut.
- It is a good idea for children to understand how to use their first-aid kits and what to do if they cut themselves. Teach them this: apply pressure – elevate – pack wound.
- Your knife is your responsibility.
- Focus and take your time.
- Rest if your hands get tired.
- Always put the knife in its sheath; never dig it into the ground or a log.

Safe ways to grip a knife

When carving, we work with the part of the blade closest to the handle. We usually mark the knife blade with a whiteboard pen, about 1in (2.5cm) away from the handle. This gives a visual indicator of the working part.

Fist grip

This is the best way to hold your knife securely and will give you confidence in each cut or carving.

Push cut

A push cut can be used for small cuts in a very controlled manner.

Knee brace

The knee brace is a very safe and controlled way to use a knife but it takes getting used to.

Splitting a stick

There are many reasons why you may need to split a stick, for example, to place in an arrow tip, to cook fish or meat on a fire, or to use for weaving. Splitting a stick with a knife in the correct form is very safe. We use two methods.

Method 1

Start with a fist grip but use your thumb and forefinger to grip the wood and apply downward pressure while rocking the knife back and forth. The knife will only go as deep as the blade.

Method 2

Start by placing the blade on the stick and then baton your knife down. Once the split is about 6in (15cm) long, take out the knife and resheath it. Then split the rest by hand. If the split wanders off-centre, bend the thicker side to bring it back on track.

Sharpening a knife

There's a saying that you are only as sharp as your knife. A blunt knife is a hazard, so keeping it sharp and well looked after is essential.

AGE 7+
TIME 5–10 minutes
TOOLS Diamond sharpening stone, flat surface (table or chopping board), old leather belt
MATERIALS Piece of paper

Step 1
For knife sharpening we mainly focus on the bevel. This is the part of the blade that angles down towards the cutting edge (see drawing on page 114). Remove metal from both sides of the bevel in order to form a fine edge where they meet. Find a flat surface to work on. If you are outdoors, a chopping block is ideal.

Step 2
Start with the knife placed on the end of the stone nearest to you. With the cutting edge facing away from you, tilt the knife until you achieve the correct bevel angle. Place your knife flat on your sharpening stone, then tilt the knife towards the cutting edge until the bevel is lying flat on the stone.

Step 3
Move the knife away from you up the stone, applying gentle pressure with your fingers. Do this twice from the bottom to the top. Turn the knife over and repeat. At this point, focus on sharpening the blade from the handle through to the first two-thirds of the blade. Sharpen the tip separately. Repeat this process on both sides, approximately 10–20 times on each side, depending on how blunt your knife is.

Step 4
To sharpen the tip, put it on the sharpening stone with the bevel lying flush and push through to the tip. Repeat on each side about 10–20 times. As you remove metal, you create a very thin burr where the bevels meet. This is formed by pushing the metal one way then the other as you alternate strokes. If you run your thumb down the bevel (towards the sharp edge, not away from it) you can feel this catch on your thumb. To see the burr, turn towards the light and check for reflections from flat spots that show any blunt areas. A sharp edge will reflect very little light.

Step 5
To smooth the edge and remove any remaining burrs, strop your knife using a leather belt. Sit on a tree stump or chair, attach the belt around your foot and hold the tail end in your other hand. Brush the knife backwards and forwards. Alternate the stropping strokes back and forth. Around 50 strokes is usually enough.

Step 6
Your knife should now feel razor-sharp. A final test of sharpness is to slice the edge off a sheet of paper.

Check your technique

Where metal has been removed from the bevel it will show as scratches or shiny areas. If your technique is correct, you will see metal has been removed from the whole bevel. If not, adjust the angles as necessary. You can draw on your knife with a permanent black pen, colouring in the bevel so that you can clearly see if your technique is even. The pen mark should be removed evenly from the entire bevel.

Carving a butter knife

This is a great activity to practise your carving techniques and strengthen your carving muscles. Carving is a great way to focus the mind while learning a new set of skills. Even the wildest group of kids can become quiet and focused when given the task of whittling a butter knife.

AGE 7+

TIME 1 hour minimum

TOOLS Fixed-blade knife

MATERIALS Piece of green hazel (*Corylus avellana*) or sycamore (*Acer pseudoplatanus*), thumb-width and as long as from your wrist to the top of your middle finger

KNIFE TECHNIQUES Fist grip, push cut and knee brace (see page 115)

Step 1
Using the fist grip, start carving the stick, taking off small slivers of wood on one side. You can use the knee brace cut to help remove larger pieces.

Step 2
Turn over the stick and carve the other side, taking off small slivers and being careful not to cut too close to the pith (centre of the stick). Always carve away from your gripping hand.

Step 3
Carve a rounded curve using the push cut at the tip of the butter knife.

Step 4
Turn the butter knife around and carve the handle, rounding the ends with a push cut.

3

4

Leave the wooden blade to dry for about a week in a cool place, then sand.

WILDERNESS SURVIVAL

Whether at home or out and about in the woods, knowing how to deal with accidents or danger will make you feel safer and more confident in any situation and increase the chances of a happy outcome. Knowing how to use the materials and equipment around you is not only useful but fun to learn, too.

Making stretchers

Making these stretchers fosters teamwork and communication as well as the challenge of making the stretchers. Give the group a scenario that includes a rescue mission where they have to make a stretcher and carry a casualty.

AGE 6+
TIME 45 mins+
TOOLS None
MATERIALS Tarp, rope, two jackets, two strong poles 7ft (2.1m) long, roll mat
KNOTS Clove hitch (see page 54)

Jacket stretcher

Step 1
Lay two poles down next to each other. Do the jackets up and pull the arms inside. Insert the poles into the arms, repeating with more jackets if necessary until the poles are covered.

Step 2
You can now carry your casualty to safety.

To make a longer stretcher, simply add more jackets to the poles.

Tarp stretcher

Step 1

Lay out the tarp. Place a pole across the width of your tarp two-thirds from one end and then fold the other third of tarp back over the pole.

Step 2

Place a second pole up against the edge of the tarp where it has been folded in and then fold the remaining third of tarp back over both poles. You are now ready to carry the injured person.

Rope stretcher

Step 1
Lay down two strong poles about an arm's length apart on the ground. Tie a clove hitch at one end of the poles. Take the rope over and under each pole so it forms a zigzag.

Step 2
Finish with another clove hitch and lay the roll mat on top of the rope. You can now carry your casualty to safety.

1

2

Plants for wilderness first aid

There are many plants around us that we can use to help heal ourselves. Knowing which ones you can use and what to do with them can mean easing a nettle or bee sting quickly, or slowing down a bleeding wound.

SAFETY
If you're not absolutely sure what something is, DO NOT pick it.

Plantain
(Plantago major)

A common weed that can be found in gardens, grasslands and roadsides. The leaves are green, egg-shaped and grow in a rosette with thick stems that meet at a base. With its antibacterial and anti-inflammatory properties, plantain is great for healing wounds, soothing burns, bringing down swelling and for treating bites or stings. Pick the leaves, chew up in your mouth or crush with a splash of cold water and apply to the affected area. This is called a compress and works immediately on nettle stings.

Plantain is better than dock leaves for soothing nettle stings. Get to know this useful plant and you will see it everywhere.

Also known as 'knitbone', comfrey is thought to help heal broken bones.

With its antibacterial, analgesic and anti-haemorrhagic (sealing of blood vessels) properties, yarrow can help stop minor wounds from bleeding. It also numbs pain and speeds up healing. Pick and crush leaves by hand and pack them onto the wound. You can use a bandage to hold them in place.

Comfrey

Comfrey is believed to help heal burns, sprains, swelling and bruises when used externally. Use only the leaves and do not use on open wounds.

Daisy

Daisies can help speed up the healing process for bruising and sprains. They are said to be anti-inflammatory and can help to reduce mild pain (but do not use on broken skin).

Common yarrow
(Achillea millefolium)

This common weed grows freely in grassland and roadsides. The leaves look like feathery ferns and the tiny white flowers form clusters at the top of the plant.

Signal fire

This is a great activity that is quick and fun but could be a vital piece of knowledge in a survival situation. Pretend you are lost in the wilderness: the only way to be found is by making a signal fire. Lots of green grasses and leaves will make thick smoke.

AGE 5+
TIME 20 minutes
TOOLS Fire steel
MATERIALS Cotton wool, silver birch bark, grasses or green leaves, small dry sticks and thin twigs made into a big bundle

Step 1
Lay your sticks down on the ground in a criss-cross pattern. Make sure you are in a safe area to light this fire, with nothing hanging from above and at least 6ft (2m) away from any tree.

Step 2
Place the cotton wool on top of the sticks and then the silver birch bark around it. Finish off with the big bundle of twigs.

Step 3
Cover it all over with the green leaves.

Step 4
Light the cotton wool with the fire steel and watch the smoke rise and become very thick

Thick smoke can be seen for miles and will help people searching to find you more quickly if you are lost.

Precautions
Be aware that a signal fire will create thick smoke that could cause a hazard to other people. Make sure you are not right next to a road and always ask the landowner's permission before making a fire.

FOREST SCHOOL HANDBOOK

PRIMITIVE SKILLS

Our ancient ancestors invented most of the basic tools we use today. Their methods were much simpler than ours and they could only use the materials they had available around them. Many of our modern tools make everyday tasks much quicker, but sometimes learning and mastering the process by hand is the real skill. It may take a whole day to achieve a finished project but the level of satisfaction in completing the process is so rewarding. After all, our hands are the best tools we own.

Slate arrow

Here we show you how to use slate to make an arrow tip that can be secured onto a stick with pine pitch glue. These days, most of us don't need to hunt to survive, but we can still enjoy the art, skill and fun involved in using a bow and arrow, as long as we know how to use them safely.

AGE 7+
TIME 30 minutes minimum
TOOLS Sharp stone for scoring the shape, hard stone for hammering, sandstone or other abrasive rock, knife
MATERIALS Piece of slate (approx. 2 x 2in/5 x 5cm and $^1/_8$in/3mm thick), hazel stick (approx. 18in/45cm long and $^3/_8$in/1cm diameter), pine pitch glue (see page 134)

> ### Tip
> Slate sheets are easy to find. Many builders' merchants have broken ones that they sometimes give away for free. Use the thinner sheets, as the thick ones have multiple layers that can be harder to work with.

Step 1

Find a hammer stone. This is round, heavy stone that is harder than the slate. Place the slate on a hard surface with the bits you wish to break off overhanging. Use the hammer stone to tap pieces of slate off until you have a rough arrow shape.

Step 2

Depending on where you live, sandstone can be easy to find once you know where to look for it. It can be pinkish in colour, sometimes crumbly and is often found in woodlands. Any abrasive rock will also work, even an old brick. Use it like sandpaper, smoothing down rough edges until you have an arrow shape.

Step 3

Cut a step into the thinner end of the hazel stick. Cut about one third of the way through the thickness of the stick $3/4$in

(2cm) from the end. Carve from this cut towards the end using a push cut (see page 115). Reheat your pine pitch glue and dab it in the step cut. Push the slate arrowhead onto the glue to fix it on.

Step 4

Finish by tying the arrowhead down with string. When you have wrapped your string around the arrow, dab a bit of pine pitch glue on to stop it unravelling.

These slate arrows are NOT designed for hunting with – they are only models. Slate can be brittle and easily break if thrown at anything.

Pine pitch glue

Humans have used resins for thousands of years for many purposes, including waterproofing, varnishing, gluing and in medicines. It is only recently that we have started using synthetic resins. Pine pitch glue is surprisingly strong and works as well as any modern glue. The best part is that it's 100% natural and you can make it yourself!

AGE 10+

TIME 30 minutes (not including foraging for the resin)

TOOLS Pestle and mortar or large round rock, stovetop or fire, old saucepan, old sieve

MATERIALS 4 tbsp (70ml) pine resin, 4 tbsp (70ml) beeswax pastilles, 2 tbsp (35ml) ground-up fine charcoal (the finer the better)

1

2

Step 1
Finely grind the charcoal using a pestle and mortar or a large round rock. The charcoal makes the glue less sticky to touch and less brittle.

Step 2
Using a low flame and an old saucepan, place the resin in the pan to melt slowly. If you are using foraged resin, you will need to pour it through an old sieve to separate any large bits of bark or general debris. When the resin is clear, heat it up slowly again. Be careful: if the mixture overheats it could lose its best qualities.

Step 3
Slowly add the beeswax pastilles. You want a 50/50 mix of resin and beeswax. This adds elasticity and makes the glue flexible.

3

Harvesting pine resin
To make pine pitch glue, you will need to harvest or source some pine resin. Pine trees produce resin to heal themselves when they have been damaged or when a branch has been broken off. It seals over wounds and protects the tree from infections and pests. The resin looks like yellowish sugar crystals and feels tacky. Quite often when you find the resin it will be dry; therefore you should be able to break it off easily, either with your fingers or with a stick.

The cleaner your resin, the stronger the glue will be.

Step 4
Take the mixture off the heat. Let it cool slightly, then add the charcoal.

Step 5
Once the mixture is well combined, find a stick and allow the mixture to collect and cool layer by layer around it, in a sort of gluey version of candyfloss. Allow it to cool completely. It should cool to a solid form on your stick. The stick can then be heated when you wish to use the glue, dabbing on a little at a time.

4

5

Using pine pitch glue

Pine pitch glue can be used for many different things, including sticking feathers on arrows or fixing arrow heads on spears. It is so useful it can be used for almost anything that you want to patch or glue in the woods.

As an alternative to charcoal, you could use sawdust, ground eggshells, bone dust, animal hair or even ground-up rabbit poop (don't use the kitchen pestle and mortar for this!).

Atl atl and spear

An atl atl is a spear thrower that our ancestors used to hunt with. The spear is attached to the atl atl and launched into the air, much like the device that dog owners use to throw balls long distances.

AGE 7+

TIME 30 minutes

TOOLS Knife (see page 114 for knife safety)

MATERIALS Hazel: one spear 5ft (1.5m) long and one stick that looks like a number 7, feathers, string, pine pitch glue (see page 134)

1

Step 1

Cut two pieces of hazel: one that looks like a number 7 and a spear that is 5ft (1.5m) long.

Step 2

Carve a point on the spear (long stick) using your carving knife. Making sure you are a safe distance from anyone else and in a safe sitting position with your elbows firmly on your knees. Use the fist grip (see page 115) to take off wood all the way around on one end of the stick to make it pointed. Don't jam the knife in; just take off small bits at a time.

2

Step 3

Make two push cuts (see page 115) opposite each other, leaving a flap of wood for the feathers to fit in. Make these at the opposite end to the point of the spear.

Step 4

Heat your pine pitch glue and attach your feather into the flaps of wood.

Step 5

Tie your string around the base of the feathers and over the glue. Use a dab of glue to hold your string in place.

Step 6

For the atl atl itself (the 'number 7' stick), cut it to arm's length and sharpen the point of the smaller branch (the tip of the number 7) using the same safe technique you used to make your spear. This is where the spear attaches. You will need to push this number 7 end slightly into the non-pointed end of your spear so there is a little indent in which it can sit.

Fat lamps

Thousands of years ago, fat lamps were used to create light in dark caves for our Stone Age ancestors. They continued to be used into the nineteenth century and beyond.

AGE 7+
TIME 10+ minutes
TOOLS Just your hands!
MATERIALS Air-dry clay, a fat source such as coconut oil, lard or sunflower oil, jute string, lighter/match

Step 1

You will need a small ball of clay, about the size of a lemon. With one hand supporting the bottom of the ball, push your thumb in the middle to make an indent. Use your thumb and forefinger to pinch and bring up the sides to make a pot shape. Smooth away any cracks with a dab of water. Too much water will collapse the pot though, so go easy. Thin out the walls, making sure they are reasonably thick at the top of the pot so it is sturdy.

Step 2

Gently pinch a lip into which the wick can sit to be able to draw up the fat. To do this, first slightly moisten the area where you are making the lip. Using two fingers, pull the clay out gently into a small-channelled spout. Support the rest of the pot while doing this so as not to split the bottom.

Step 3

Choose your oil. I like coconut oil: it has many different uses including as a fuel. It will burn well even in solid form. Otherwise, lard and sunflower oil are good, too. You can add the oil in solid form; it does not have to be melted or liquid, as this will happen as it burns. Half-fill your pot with your chosen oil. Lay the wick in the oil, with one end resting on the spouted lip.

Step 4

Use your fingers to lightly dab some oil on the exposed end of the wick and then light it. The wick should now draw the oil up and remain lit until the oil burns out.

Ancient light

Archaeologists have found limestone and sandstone rocks chipped away to create a small dip in which oil would have been burnt, and these date back at least 40,000 years. Our Stone Age ancestors would not have wasted anything, especially when using animals for survival. They would have used the fat to burn in their lamps.

Fat lamps have been found in caves along with ancient cave art. It is believed that, with the use of torches and fat lamps, the images would appear more alive. With the glow of a flickering light, deer would leap, horses would run and hunters with spears would vibrate with life. Along with an excitable storyteller, these pictures might have been like early movies!

1

2

3

4

Tip

You can use different materials for wick: moss, jute, string, various barks (pounded, softened and twisted), cotton wool or grasses. Rosebay, willow or sedge grass will work, as these have a spongy centre that when pre-soaked in oil stays alight for around 20 minutes.

PRIMITIVE SKILLS

143

Nut lamps

Nuts and seeds offer us useful oils for cooking (sesame, walnut, sunflower, etc.), but they can also be used to make little lamps. If you're anything like me, you don't go anywhere without a bag of trail mix, so will always have the materials you need to make one.

AGE 6+
TIME 10 minutes preparation
TOOLS Pounding rock, wooden chopping board or flat rock, lighter or matches
MATERIALS Nuts with a high oil content such as walnuts, pecans, hazelnuts or Brazil nuts

Step 1

Choose your nuts – the fresher the better and in their shells if possible. You only need two or three for each lamp. Find a flat rock or chopping board. You'll need a good, round pounding stone for this next part. With the shells taken off, crush up the nuts into a fine paste. If they are fresh enough you should start to see the oils coming out pretty quickly.

Step 2

Once the nuts have been pounded into a paste, form the paste into a small pyramid shape on the flat rock or chopping board and light the top. It's as simple as that. You will be amazed at how long they burn!

Grass mat

*Sometimes, on a cold day when a sit spot calls, or if I'm
going camping or spending time outdoors, especially after
rainfall, I wish I had something to sit on: something that
I didn't have to worry about getting dirty or wet, and
something light to carry and easy to pack in a rucksack.
A woven grass mat is a perfect solution. It's easy to make,
easy to transport and easy to replace when necessary.*

AGE 6+
TIME 1 hour
TOOLS Saw, secateurs,
scissors, knife
MATERIALS Hazel sticks x
7, 2ft (60cm) long, plenty
of long grass, string or
paracord

Stone Age weaving
Our Stone Age ancestors would have been keen
weavers, using the fibres of plants and the hides and
sinews of animals to weave to create the necessities of
life. Weaving a grass mat is one way we can recreate
their experience.

FOREST SCHOOL HANDBOOK

You can use other grasses and reeds, and even hay or straw if you don't have access to long grass.

Step 1

Push some straight sticks into the ground to make the weaving loom. Use at least six sticks of about 2ft (60cm) long. Position each stick so it has a pair on the opposite side. The distance between the pairs is determined by the size you want your project to be. For a simple sit mat I would recommend they are 2ft 6in (76cm) apart.

Step 2

Tie a length of string or cord between each pair to connect them. This is the 'weft'.

Step 3

Tie an additional length of string to each stick on one side, but do not connect to the opposite pair. Instead, connect the loose ends to another stick. This is the weaving bar; it should be a few inches longer than the width of the row of stakes.

Step 4

Lift the weaving bar up above the weft to reveal a gap. Place long bundles of your chosen fibre on top of the weft and lower the weaving bar. This becomes the 'warp'.

Step 5

Repeat by alternately lifting and lowering the weaving bar, adding more warp fibres each time. The closer together the warp, the stronger and thicker your mat will be. When it has reached the desired thickness, cut the string attached to the weaving bar and carefully lift the mat off the loom.

Making a coil pot

If you are working with clay for the first time, I would recommend using air-dry clay as it requires no firing to harden it. Whether you are using natural clay without firing (see page 34 for details on how to source it) or air-dry clay, your creations will turn back to clay if left outside in the elements.

AGE 7+

TIME 1 hour+

TOOLS Water, sponge, sticks, feathers/comb to make patterns, hard surface such as a chopping board

MATERIALS Air-dry (or natural) clay

Step 1

To make the base, take a ball of clay about the size of a ping-pong ball. Flatten it with the palm of your hand. Insert your thumb into the centre to make an indent and thin out the walls with your thumb and forefinger so it looks like a small dish.

Step 2

Take another piece of clay about the same size as the first. Roll it out on a hard surface to make a long worm shape for your first coil. Slightly moisten the rim of the base but not too much as this will make the pot too wet to handle and it could start to collapse.

Step 3

Place the coil around the edge of the base. Very carefully, smooth down the edges of the join to hide it. Repeat, adding the next coil on top. You can choose whether to keep the coils separate on the inside or smooth these out, too.

Step 4

Add as many coils as you like to build up the walls of your pot. When it is the desired size, take three times the amount of clay used for your first coils to make the last coil. This time, once you have rolled it out, flatten it slightly with your forefinger to make a slab around 3/8in (1cm) thick.

Step 5

Adding a little water, attach it to the inside of your pot at the top, overlapping the edges. Gently press the walls into the slab so that they join tightly. Allow the top part of the slab to curve outwards, making the lip of the pot by gently bending it out.

Tip

- If you leave the pot to dry for around 10–15 minutes after every two to three layers of coils, it is easier to build on, as the clay starts to harden slightly. Add a little water to help join your pieces together.

- If it has been joined well and is thick enough, once the pot is completely dry, the lip made in step 5 could be used to lift the pot from a fire using a stick either side.

1

2

3

4

5

Decorate your pot by making indents using sticks, feathers, shells and whatever else you can find.

Cave art and natural paints

Early humans created cave art thousands of years ago using pigments made from charcoal, blood, mud, clays and ochres. These pigments were then made into a paint or paste with various binders, including water, vegetable juices, urine, animal fat, bone marrow, blood and egg whites. They might have painted these images to communicate with one another, retelling epic tales of gruelling hunts and other adventures. Why not find yourself a large rock, or some slate or brown paper to experiment with natural paints?

Ochre paints

Ochres are natural earth pigments that contain iron oxide, creating a range of reds, oranges, yellows and browns. You can buy them easily online or, if you are lucky, can sometimes source some by breaking open rocks. They can be mixed with water or with oils to create different effects. Use a shell, a rock or an old plastic pot to mix ochres with water to make a paste. You can also make a type of oil pastel by adding animal fat to ochre pigment powder. Try adding a teaspoon of lard to your paste to recreate this effect.

Charcoal

Charcoal can be crushed between rocks and ground down to make a powder and used either on its own as a pencil, mixed with water, or with lard or other fat. Charcoal can be bought from art supply shops, but you can also make your own (see page 90).

Stone Age artists may have achieved spray effects by blowing paint through hollow bones.

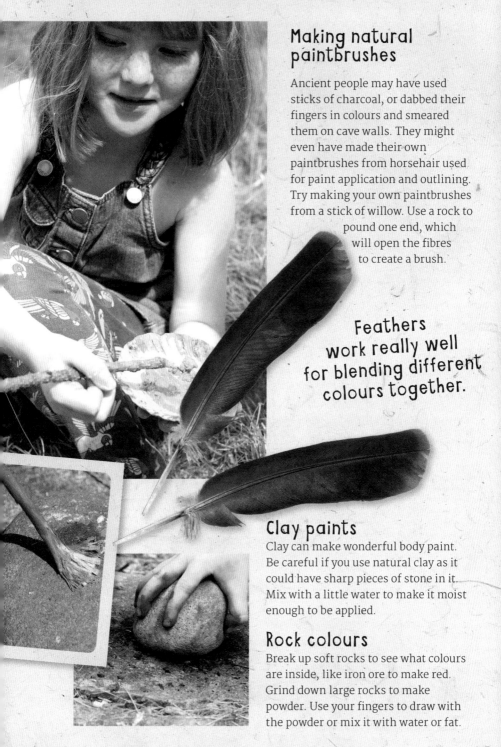

Making natural paintbrushes

Ancient people may have used sticks of charcoal, or dabbed their fingers in colours and smeared them on cave walls. They might even have made their own paintbrushes from horsehair used for paint application and outlining. Try making your own paintbrushes from a stick of willow. Use a rock to pound one end, which will open the fibres to create a brush.

Feathers work really well for blending different colours together.

Clay paints

Clay can make wonderful body paint. Be careful if you use natural clay as it could have sharp pieces of stone in it. Mix with a little water to make it moist enough to be applied.

Rock colours

Break up soft rocks to see what colours are inside, like iron ore to make red. Grind down large rocks to make powder. Use your fingers to draw with the powder or mix it with water or fat.

WILD FOOD

There's nothing more delicious or satisfying than a meal sourced from nature. When you know what to look for, you'll soon see that at the right time of year mother nature provides us with a fabulous feast for the picking. Hedgerows and woodlands are great places to forage for food and medicinal plants. You can find edible plants that can be made into delicious meals and snacks. Some can even be cooked on the campfire and enjoyed while sitting around it.

Foraging safely

Foraging for food can be both engaging and educational. There are few things more satisfying than bringing a basket of foraged food to the table. Learning to identify what is what, where it grows, what it looks like and which parts are edible is all part of the enjoyment. Even if you are looking for the most common, well-known plants, there are still lots of things to consider before you go out picking.

Foraging checklist

Foraging can be great fun, as well as delicious, but always be careful when out picking. Ask yourself these simple questions before you pick anything:

- Am I completely sure that it is what I think it is?
- Do I need permission to pick here?
- Is there plenty for me to pick and still leave some to grow?
- Am I picking for a purpose?
- Is this a safe area to pick from?

If the answer is not 'yes' to every one of these questions, then rethink and don't pick. If you are not 100% positive, don't pick them.

Foraging tips

- Always try a little before you try a lot. Even when classed as edible, that doesn't always mean that your body will react in a positive way.
- Wear long trousers and long-sleeved tops to protect from brambles and nettles.
- Carry a small first-aid kit and a bottle of water.
- Take a small basket with you so as not to crush your delicious edibles in a bag.
- Make sure you go foraging with a responsible adult.

Identifying correctly

Never assume that you know a plant. Have more than three identification features. Do not use smell alone as scent can transfer to your hands from another plant.

REMEMBER: if you're not 100% sure what it is, DO NOT PICK. You can either come back with a reference book later or bring someone who can identify the plant.

Plants to know

These three common plants can be used in the recipes that follow in this section. Get to know them well before you think about harvesting and follow the advice on page 153.

Dandelion
(Taraxacum)

Dandelions are a wonder herb that most people think of as a weed. Their fluffy seedhead and jagged green leaves grow in blankets in meadows and in gardens. The leaves contain vitamins A, C and K, and are good sources of calcium, potassium and iron. The flowers are a vibrant yellow and orange and turn into fluffy white seedheads.

Nettles
(Urtica dioica)

Nettles can be found pretty much everywhere, in fields, woodlands and roadsides. They have many healing properties including being very high in vitamin C and iron. The dark green, heart-shaped leaves are jagged and pointy like a giant teardrop. The stem is thick and finely haired. The flowers grow in clusters of tiny seeds hanging from the stem.

Wild garlic
(Allium ursinum)

Wild garlic, also known as ramsons, is a member of the onion family. The leaves and flowers are edible. Young leaves, appearing in March, are delicious added to soups, sauces and pesto. The flowers can add a potent garlicky punch to salads. It mainly grows in ancient woodland and on river banks and is known for its antibacterial qualities and contains vitamins A and C, calcium and iron. Bright, star-like white flowers grow in vibrant clusters, often creating a blanket on the woodland floor. The leaves are long, shiny and pointy, growing in pairs.

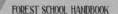

Preparing nettles

Nettles are, in my opinion, under-appreciated. Yes they can sting, but why not bite them before they bite you? They are delicious and very nutritious. Full of vitamins, calcium, potassium and iron, and high in protein. The best part is that they grow abundantly and are completely free.

Picking and cleaning

To avoid getting stung, wear long-sleeved tops and trousers and gloves when harvesting. You can use scissors and cut directly into a bowl to avoid having to handle them at all. Pick the first two or three pairs of leaves from the tops of the plants as these will be the most tender. Carefully place the nettles into a bag or container for transporting.

Clean the nettles by swishing them around (wearing gloves) in a large sink or basin filled with cool water. Lift the nettles out, leaving any grit behind, and drain them.

What takes the sting out of a nettle?

- Cooking or pouring boiling-hot water over them.
- Crushing them.
- Letting them wilt.
- Dehydrating them and letting them dry to a crisp over a few weeks, or in a dehydrator.
- Blending them into a sauce, paste or smoothie.

Nettle crisps

Ingredients
- Young nettle leaves
- 2 tbsp oil of your choice
- 1 tsp salt
- 1 tsp crushed red pepper flakes (optional)
- 1 tsp freshly ground pepper
- 2 tbsp nutritional yeast flakes (optional but highly recommended, available at most supermarkets and health food shops)

Wear gloves to handle the leaves as they will still have their sting until they are cooked.

Step 1
Strip the nettle leaves from the stems. Wash and dry them, patting them gently with a tea towel.

Step 2
Combine all the seasoning ingredients and oil, including the nutritional yeast flakes if you are using them, in a large bowl and toss in the leaves, making sure they get a good coating.

Step 3
Place the nettles on a baking sheet in a single layer. DO NOT be tempted to try one yet.

Step 4
Bake in a low oven at around 250°F (130°C) until they are crisp, turning once halfway through. This should take about 25 minutes. How long they take will depend on how much moisture there is in the leaves. When cool, place in a bowl and devour.

Nettle smoothie

Ingredients
- 1 banana
- ¼ pineapple
- 3 tbsp coconut milk
- ¼ cucumber (peeled and cubed)
- ½ avocado, for a creamier smoothie (optional)
- 1 handful nettle leaves

Step 1
You can either clean the nettles (see page 155) and use them immediately, or let them wilt overnight to reduce the sting.

Step 2
Add all the ingredients to a blender and whizz really well. Make sure to blend long enough to end up with a smooth mixture. The nettles need to be shredded completely to ensure they will no longer sting.

Nettle energy balls

Ingredients

- 8oz (225g) dates
- 4oz (110g) soaked sunflower seeds (soak 3oz/85g of dried sunflower seeds and leave overnight, drain and rinse, then leave for a few hours to dry slightly)
- 6 tsp (35ml) chopped raw nettle leaves
- 1–2 tsp (5–10ml) coconut oil
- ½ tbsp (8ml) cocoa powder
- 1 tsp (5ml) cinnamon (optional)
- 1 tsp (5ml) dried nori flakes (optional – this gives a strong and unique taste but adds iron)
- 2 tsp (10ml) desiccated coconut

FOR THE TOPPING:
- 1 tbsp (15ml) desiccated coconut

Step 1
Blend the soaked sunflower seeds and the chopped raw nettles in a food processor with an S-blade until roughly chopped.

Step 2
Add the remaining ingredients to the food processor and blend again until the mixture resembles fine crumbs.

Step 3
Take small scoops of the mixture and roll them into balls using the palms of your hands.

The foraged nettles won't be able to sting once they have been chopped up in the food processor.

Step 4
Roll each ball in desiccated coconut. Put them into the refrigerator for an hour or so, or as long as it takes for them to firm up. Once they are firm, store in an airtight container.

Wild garlic and walnut pesto

Ingredients
- 5 wild garlic leaves
- Small bunch of mint leaves
- Small bunch of basil leaves
- Handful of walnuts
- 1¾oz (50g) Parmesan cheese
- Pinch of salt and pepper
- Generous dash of olive oil
- Juice of half a lemon

Step 1
Find a patch of wild garlic and pick a small bunch of leaves. Wash them well.

Step 2
Put all the ingredients into a blender and whizz them thoroughly.

Step 3
Taste test and season to your liking, adding more salt or pepper as desired.

Step 4
Empty the contents into pots with lids and store in the fridge. This will keep for up to five days. It is great with pasta, added to roast vegetables and as a delicious alternative for a pizza base sauce.

Ash breads

Ingredients
- 6oz (175g) self-raising flour
- A few splashes of water
- These breads are cooked on a campfire (see page 85–87)

Step 1
Mix the flour with a few splashes of water. Too much water and your dough will be too gooey; too little and you will end up with breadcrumbs. The dough should hold together but not stick to your hands. Keep adding flour and water until you get the right mix, using your hands to squidge it together.

Step 2
Break the dough up into pieces the size of ping-pong balls and squash them between the palms of your hands. Place them directly onto the coals of a campfire. If the coals are nice and hot your bread should cook in just a minute each side. Keep turning until golden on each side (don't worry if they burn a little; this just adds to the flavour). Check that they are cooked all the way through by breaking one open. Eat with lashings of chocolate spread for a delicious treat!

Cheesy bread twists
Make the dough in the same way, adding some grated cheese. Using your hands, squish the dough into long sausages. Twist one around the end of a green stick about 39in (1m) long, hazel or sycamore work well.

Hold the stick next to the fire for 10–15 minutes, while the bread cooks. Keep turning it so it turns golden-brown all around. When it is cooked it will sound hollow when you tap it.

Dandelion cookies

Ingredients
- ½ cup butter, softened
- ½ cup 100% peanut butter
- ½ cup honey
- 1 egg
- 1 tsp vanilla extract
- 1 tsp baking powder
- 1 cup plain flour
- 1 cup wholewheat flour
- ½ cup dandelion petals

Dandelions are best picked during the autumn or spring when they are nice and tender.

Step 1
Preheat the oven to 350°F (180°C). Line a baking sheet with greaseproof paper or a silicone baking mat. Sift together the flour and baking powder and set aside.

Step 2
Cream together the butter, peanut butter and honey until light and fluffy. Beat in the egg and vanilla extract until well mixed.

Step 3
Add the dry ingredients to the butter mixture and make a soft dough. Gently fold in the dandelion petals.

Step 4
Drop spoonfuls onto the baking sheet. Bake in the preheated oven for about 15 minutes, or until golden. Cool on a wire rack.

Preparing the dandelions
Snip the petals from the flower. It's OK to get a few bits of green in the cookies but mostly you'll want the yellow petals for optimum flavour. Too much green stuff, and the cookies might take on an unpleasant bitter taste. It does take a little time, but it is worth it.

Blackberry sorbet

Ingredients
- 4 cups (560g) blackberries
- 2½ cups (600ml) water
- 2 tbsp (30ml) lemon juice
- ½–1 cup (100–200g) coconut sugar or cane sugar (you can experiment with other sweeteners too: honey, maple syrup, date syrup etc.)

Step 1
Rinse the blackberries, then combine in a blender with the water and lemon juice. Whizz until smooth, then press the mixture through a sieve and discard the seeds.

Step 2
Place the blackberry mixture and sugar in a saucepan. Bring to the boil and reduce to a simmer. Let it cook for 1–2 minutes, until the sugar is fully dissolved.

Step 3
Remove from the heat, transfer into a container and place it in the refrigerator to chill completely.

Step 4
Once it has cooled down, pour the mixture into a shallow pan and place in a freezer for approximately 1 hour, or until frozen solid. Once frozen, break it into pieces and whizz in a blender or food processor until creamy and freeze again for 20 minutes. This process breaks up the ice crystals to give a smoother sorbet.

Try adding some herbs or spices, ginger perhaps (fresh or dried) or maybe some mint leaves, during the boiling process. Let your taste buds guide you.

Toffee apples

Ingredients
- Apples
- Brown sugar
- Cinnamon (optional)
- The toffee apples are cooked over a campfire (see page 85–87)

Step 1
Peel the apple and sharpen one end of a long stick.

Step 2
Mix up a handful of brown sugar with a sprinkling of cinnamon and keep to one side.

Step 3
Skewer the apple on the sharp end of the stick. Cook over the fire, turning frequently. It's ready when it starts to bubble all over.

Step 4
Be careful, as it will be very hot! Roll in your sugar mix until completely covered. Cook on the fire again, rotating frequently until all the sugar has completely melted. Wait until the toffee has cooled and then eat.

Index

First published 2023 by Guild of Master Craftsman Publications Ltd, Castle Place, 166 High Street, Lewes, East Sussex, BN7 1XU, United Kingdom. Text © Naomi Walmsley and Dan Westall, 2023. Copyright in the Work © GMC Publications Ltd, 2023. This book was created using material from *Forest School Adventure*, first published 2018, and *Urban Forest School,* first published 2020. ISBN 978 1 78494 665 4. All rights reserved.
A catalogue record for this book is available from the British Library.

Publisher Jonathan Bailey
Production Director Jim Bulley
Design Manager Robin Shields
Senior Project Editor Virginia Brehaut
Designer Lynne Lanning
Illustrator Sarah Skeate (including cover)

Colour origination by GMC Reprographics.
Printed and bound in China

Picture credits
All photos by Dan Westall and Rachel Walmsley, except the following from Shutterstock.com on pages: 4–5 (cut outs), 8 (top and bottom), 13 (cut outs), 22–23 (cut outs), 24 (bottom left and right), 26, 27 (middle), 30–31 (middle bottom), 40–41 (cut outs), 42 (lower), 43 (right), 48 (left, middle, bottom right), 49 (top left, bottom right), 67 (top left), 70, 71 (bottom), 73 (cut outs), 74 (top right), 81, 100, 101 (bottom), 104 (bottom), 105 (bottom), 107, 108, 119 (bottom), 126–127 (all), 128, 131 (bottom), 135 (bottom), 143 (bottom, left, right), 145 (bottom), 150 (left), 151 (cut out), 152, 153, 154, 155 (bottom), 159, (bottom), 161.

GMC Publications Ltd
Castle Place, 166 High Street,
Lewes, East Sussex,
BN7 1XU
United Kingdom
Tel: +44 (0)1273 488005

www.gmcbooks.com